WORKED

A Bench Guide to Hand-Tool Efficiency

Joshua A. Klein

Mortise & Tenon Inc.

SEDGWICK

Author
Joshua A. Klein

Editor
Michael Updegraff

Copy Editor
Kara Gebhart Uhl

Photographer and Designer
Joshua A. Klein

Publisher
Mortise & Tenon

Image opposite title page: Pehr Hilleström, "En Snickare," 1794.

ISBN: 978-1-7365627-4-1

Mortise & Tenon Inc.
14 Porcupine Ln
Sedgwick, ME 04676

www.mortiseandtenonmag.com

Printed and bound in the United States of America

Signature Book Printing
8041 Cessna Ave
Gaithersburg, MD 20879

www.sbpbooks.com

CONTENTS

For Eden, Asher, and Wyeth.
May you long enjoy the work of your hands.

Rethinking 'Efficiency'

At the outset of this book, I have to confess that I have come to develop misgivings about the word "efficiency" in relation to handcraft. On the one hand, it is a good thing to avoid squandering resources (time, wood, energy, etc.) in our productive efforts. There are ways to maximize the usefulness of a board, just like there are occasions when we need to get the most out of our shop time. This is a good and noble aim.

At the same time, a focus on completing a project "as soon as possible" tends to eclipse the very reason so many of us pick up saw, plane, and chisel in the first place. Somehow the process is overshadowed by the product. This hustle-and-bustle way of life has infected most of us in the 21st century. For hundreds of years, we moderns have conditioned ourselves to *production*, above all else. Today, we want crash courses, life hacks, and seven simple steps to success. We want to see *results* apart from the patient cultivation of skill.

Now, I've been trying to shake myself of this mentality for a while, and I will say it's not been easy. Not "wasting" time on inefficient methods and always seeking to expedite the task at hand has framed much of my woodworking. In talking to other craftspeople, I get the feeling I may not be the only one. Whether you're a hand-tool nut or a power-tool devotee (or something in between), we all can be tempted to think this way. If a given method of work is faster, it's better by definition, we think.

But what if woodworking wasn't about getting it over with as soon as possible? What if we picked up tools because we actually enjoyed the process of skillfully shaping wood? How relevant would this impulse for "efficiency" be then?

Maybe our notion of the thing needs a little revision.

Usually when I hear woodworkers talk about "being efficient," they're referring to *economic* efficiency. What they're focused on is the time invested to procure a given output. And even those who aren't looking to peddle their wares often think like a professional: "I would lose my shirt doing it that way!" But if there's no shirt on the line, then there's no shirt to lose.

A little etymological digging reveals an even deeper, more basic meaning of this word. In the old sense, "efficient" simply meant "to cause an effect." *An American Dictionary of the English Language* (Webster's 1828) defines it: "Causing effects; producing; that causes any thing to be what it is. The *efficient* cause is that which produces; the final cause is that for which it is produced." In the noun form, the efficient is "the agent which produces." Notice how this definition is not bound up with a huffing-and-puffing obsession with meeting a deadline or minimizing labor. It's not fixated on getting it out the door ASAP. It's not driven by the bottom line or the sales report.

I find this old notion of "efficiency" refreshing. And the good news is that this sense of the word is not *totally* extinct. The *Oxford English Dictionary* tells us that efficiency is "fitness or power to accomplish, or success in accomplishing, the purpose intended; adequate power, effectiveness, efficacy." So, efficiency is about fitness, or competence, to accomplish an intended aim. How close can you hew to that line without spoiling the piece? How handily can you wield that chisel as you pare a chamfer? Watch any experienced craftsperson at work, and you will see them make it look easy, though they never look rushed. *That* is craftsmanship.

The approach I set forth in this book is not efficiency for efficiency's sake, but it is efficiency for *proficiency's* sake. Think of when you learned to ride a bike – there's no way to learn going slow. In order to stay upright, you've got to develop at least a little bit of speed. Otherwise, you'll wobble and tip over. I have seen many beginners use hand tools so slowly that they never seem to get rolling. As we walk through these chapters, I encourage you to keep at the forefront of your mind that the kind of efficiency we're talking about here is more about *agency* and *ability* than it is labor savings.

Worked is intended to convey no-nonsense, workmanlike approaches to handwork, but it is not a cheat sheet with easy hacks and speed tips for immediate results. The book you hold in your hands is a guide to aid your own exercise of competence over the long term. It's been written for the cultivation of *skill*.

So, the assumption of this book is that the reader wants to be a craftsperson, not a factory worker; or, as another writer has put it, aims to develop the fruitfulness of a tree, not the efficiency of a machine.

I couldn't have said it better myself.

SECTION I: STOCK PREP

Putting the "work" back into woodworking...

Never forget that woodworking is nothing less than *working* wood. You will sweat and bleed. You will struggle and murmur under your breath, "There's got to be a better way to do this." And although there often is, we should not assume that something must be wrong if our heart rate begins increasing. No, work is a good thing. It's good for your muscles, good for your heart, and it's good for your soul.

Modern production methods have attempted to make the chapters I present in this book obsolete and unnecessary. Machines have replaced apprentices, and for this we are told we should all be grateful. "Why bother with people," they tell us, "when a machine will do a better job and cheaper?" They encourage us to reserve our artisanal expertise for the final touches of assembly and to let the machines do the grunt work.

I'm convinced that this mentality is often predicated on the assumption that sizing and preparing stock is nothing more than the unfortunate preliminary stage we have to "get out of the way" to get to the *actual* woodworking – you know, the *fun* part. *Who in their right mind could enjoy physical exertion?* some may wonder.

I reject this assertion.

Not only is preparing stock a substantial and essential aspect of any woodworking project, but our embrace of its physicality and intimacy of involvement with the material will stretch our capacities as artisans. To *know* wood, you have to wrestle it. To discover its secrets, you must take up the rough-sawn plank and run a razor edge down its length. There, you will find where the grain dives, how the board was oriented

The underside of the top of this 18th-century English desk was left with "traversing" (across-the-grain) fore-plane marks.

within the standing tree, and in what way the board's flat-sawn cathedrals direct you to engage it.

We must remember that fitting and assembling joinery are merely the very last stages of a journey that began long before – one that started with sleeves rolled up for action, fore plane in hand. There are many shavings and many insights that emerge between that first pass of the plane and the final fit of the joinery. So, let's not overlook these fundamental steps that inform so much of what comes after.

One 20th-century wit was rumored to have quipped, "In theory, there is no difference between practice and theory. In practice, there is." This clever turn of phrase works because we know deep down that it's one thing to hear an explanation or watch a demonstration of something, but it's quite another to actually try *your* hand at it. So, if these chapters make the craft look easy, that may just be an indication that you're on the right path. Keep at it. Nothing worth doing is easy at first.

The first section of this book is broken up into six chapters, designed to walk you through the skills involved in breaking down, smoothing, and sizing stock (boards or rounds). Though we will be using a relatively small tool kit for this sweaty work, I suspect many of my readers will lack the appropriate forms. Our tools must be workhorses, stoutly tuned, freshly sharp, and champing at the bit. Most modern woodworking tools are designed for elegant finishing work, not hearty wood removal.

We'll discuss tool particulars another day, but as an overview, you will need a 6-8 teeth-per-inch (tpi) crosscut handsaw with palpable set. Your ripsaw should be coarse – 4 tpi is my preference. Ripping with finer saws (5 or 6 tpi) will get you there eventually, but those are the saws that give hand ripping a reputation for monotonous drudgery. Ninety percent of your stock planing will be done with a fore (also known as a "jack") plane. Make sure it has a wide-open mouth to take the biggest bites your arms can manage – it'll help. Oh, and get yourself a hatchet. I intend to convince you that every woodshop needs a hewing stump and razor-sharp hatchet at the ready. There are many stock-prep instances when I find myself at the stump, but we'll come to those in time.

LEFT: The inside of a rail from an 18th-century drop-leaf table shows remnants of the rough surface from the sawmill. This board was hastily planed.

ON TOLERANCES

As I discussed in my previous book *Joined*, pre-industrial furniture making is premised on the idea that there are primary (outside or "sacred") surfaces that ought to be smooth and pretty, and secondary (inside) surfaces that don't. Though this point is absolutely *essential* to understand, modern people find it hard to accept. They smooth the insides just like the outsides and they get turned around during construction. They start looking for little smudgy pencil lines that denote the orientation of the board but end up wasting so much time flipping pieces 'round and 'round in order to make any progress. Leave the inside rough and you will never be confused about which side is which. This simple (historic) approach not only economizes our time planing stock, but it makes all our layout so much more intuitive.

ABOVE: The underside of this drop-leaf table was traversed quite aggressively. In some places, there appear to be adze marks – quite a surprising tool to use for a tabletop.

RIGHT: The back of this 18th-century drawer shows the undulations from the fore plane.

BELOW: The camber of the maker's fore plane iron matches the camber of the tool marks on his furniture.

"[W]hile it can be tempting to look at an exquisite piece of wooden furniture or temple architecture and to admire the accuracy of the planing and the precision of the joints, **the concepts of precision and accuracy can never be strictly applied to objects made of wood** – because wood is flexible; it swells and contracts in unpredictable ways; it can never be truly of a fixed dimension because by its very nature it is a substance still fixed in the natural world. Whether planed or jointed, lapped or milled, or varnished to a brilliant luster, **it is fundamentally inherently imprecise.**"

– Simon Winchester, *The Perfectionists*

Unfortunately for our aim here, we must come to grips with the fact that the subtleties of handcraft are notoriously challenging to teach by written word and a photo here or there. This is partially because the diversity of body postures cannot be captured in a handful of photographs. Woodworking is not a static thing, it's an *activity* made up of fluid motions and responsive sensual perceptions. Imagine trying to teach someone to dance, exclusively from still imagery – it's just going to be a struggle.

But the other challenge we face is the communication of appropriate tolerances. Exactly how flat is "flat?" How smooth is "smooth?" While a feeler gauge under a straightedge might get us part of the way there, any conversation about tolerances really ought to be done in person with the work at the bench. We'll do what we can, but at the end of the day, you've got to see it for yourself.

Machinists, more than anyone, know that specific jobs have specific tolerances. Some jobs need only to be accurate to .001" and others require refinement to .0000001". Every trade, every medium, and every product relates to different standards. The tolerances for NASA's rockets are meaningless to a timber framer who doesn't really need a rule of increments finer than 1/8".

So, the question is not whether our furniture making needs to be accurate – rather, "What

is 'within tolerance' for furniture?" I imagine that some of my readers initially will be disappointed to learn that every situation is different, that there is no specific decimal place value I can give you within which the dimensions of every furniture component must fall. The good news, however, is that the question is largely irrelevant – furniture must *look good* and *function properly* and nothing more. Regardless of the microscopic deviation that precision measuring devices may reveal, if it *looks* good, it *is* good. How do you know if the straight taper of your table leg is straight enough? Take a step back. How does it look? Drawers must slide in and out freely (function), but the fit of the drawer face should look good (aesthetics). Does it look sloppy, full of gaps? That is your measurement of tolerance. Tabletops do not need to be NASA flat, but you don't want a visible hollow.

In short, *your eye is the standard* of tolerance. And over the years as your hand skills develop, so will your sense of visual discernment. Dovetails that you were happy with at the beginning of your journey will undoubtedly make you wince a few years into your growth as an artisan. That's not only OK, it's expected. It's called maturation. But as you grow in the craft, don't ever forget that it's just woodworking, reader. Although the joinery of the past was intended to be as gap-free as possible, the tolerances of our furniture-making ancestors were much closer to those of house carpenters than those of space engineers.

Efficient craftsmanship is caring deeply about everything that matters and being disciplined enough to overlook everything else. It's common today for people to feel that fussing their way to a perceived perfection is somehow noble, but this can also simply be a matter of pride. Fussing over everything is not a workmanlike mindset, and I'm going to show you a different way.

If you've heard of the "Pareto Principle," also known as the "80/20 Rule," you might be able to picture the mindset I'm talking about here. The principle states that 80 percent of a perfect result is produced in 20 percent of the effort – roughing everything out is the quick part. The last 20 percent, involving finessing and fine-tuning, takes the last 80 percent of the effort – this is the tedious and fussy part. This principle, which has been applied across so many disciplines, is also true for handmade furniture. This is why vernacular furniture is often solidly constructed but rarely fussed over – Joe Farmer-Craftsman knew to avoid getting bogged down in the details. An experienced craftsperson can quickly discern when the work starts slowing down and getting picky. If you look at the insides of period furniture, you'll see that pre-industrial artisans didn't fuss where it didn't matter. There is no glory in pushing through the last 80 percent of the work to make it just a *little* bit better. Bowl maker David Pye once postulated that "half the art of workmanship" is balancing the tension between precision and artful freedom.

We've got to know when to quit.

The backboards of this 18th-century high chest of drawers are a stark contrast to its elegantly figured show faces. This guy didn't spend effort where it wouldn't count.

Sawing Rough Boards

It can be unwieldy to manage large boards, especially in a small shop space. Pre-industrial professional craftsmen rarely had luxurious and spacious shops – 12' x 18' seems to have been an average size. With the workbench (or two), tool chest, sawbench, hewing stump, and partially assembled project, there was little room for interior lumber storage. It was not uncommon for some lumber to be stored in the garret overhead, but any serious amount of board footage was carefully stacked and stickered out in the yard, covered if possible. This is my situation precisely. Until I construct a permanent shed addition, I have a temporary tarp-roofed building covering my furniture-grade lumber.

The downside to outdoor storage is that the lumber retains a slightly higher moisture content. Once the boards are brought into the shop, they tend to lose some moisture (due to heating, etc.) which can cause warpage or checking if the change is too extreme. All this to say, bring your stock into your shop well before you begin your project – if the lumber is already dry, a week is good. Even if you have to break down all your stock to fit it into your space, plan to do so. Buy a moisture meter if it makes you sleep better, but don't let the numbers distract you from paying attention to the material itself. There are no moisture charts I can give you that will perfectly fit your situation, because woodworking is more of an art than a science. You will, through experience, get to know your particular stash of wood, your area's seasonal fluctuations, and how these interact when you bring it into your shop. That's the art of it.

The very first thing to do when approaching large boards is to cut that stuff to length. Whether you have a cut list or not (I rarely do), plan your cut carefully, seeing how you might maximize the material. This does not always mean fitting as many parts as possible in one board; sometimes the beauty or configuration of the grain is more significant than avoiding waste. Regardless, it is quite common for the ends of boards to have checks from drying. After measuring to plan out your cuts, mark one end to cut.

Do everything you can to avoid dealing with knots. Boards come from trees, and trees have knots, I know. But this is not an asset to our work. Especially if you are dealing with kiln-dried material, those knots can be hard enough to chip your plane iron. But the hardness isn't even the biggest headache; it's the changing grain direction. Where the knot emerges, the grain runs together. What this means (as you'll soon find out) is that planing on one side of the knot, the grain will cut nice and clean, while the opposite side will tear horribly. Avoid knots in show surfaces as much as you can. The knottiest of the lot are best used as backboards.

Don't put your line too close to the knot as the aforementioned grain diving can kick you in the butt while planing. I make sure I have at least an inch beyond the line to the knot. I also make sure that my rough stock is sawn at least 1" longer at each end because the beginning and ending of each planed board can develop irregularities that are best sawn off at the final sizing stages. Don't forget this: All your rough stock is sawn slightly oversized.

The sawbench is an essential shop appliance for the hand-tool woodworker. You will be at this thing all the time. It can be as elaborate as you want to make it, but mine is nothing more than four sticks tenoned through a 3"-thick softwood plank. Make one longer sawbench rather than two short ones – it's a much more versatile arrangement.

This is the typical body posture for crosscutting. If you are right-handed (lefties should reverse these guidelines), use your left knee and left hand to pin the board to the bench while you saw with your right hand. This leaves your body open to sawing and offers the most comfortable sawing position. Lean most of your body weight forward onto the board to stabilize it as much as possible. You don't want that thing wobbling around.

Stability is the key here. Years back, I began wrapping my left ankle around my right leg. This ties my three points of contact (right foot, left hand, and left knee) more tightly together. If you find yourself wanting more control, give it a shot.

Starting a saw cut is a tricky thing for new woodworkers because those teeth want to grab. But there is a simple and reliable way: Use your left thumb to guide the sawplate onto the line. Once you've set the teeth on the edge of the board, drop the handle so that the toothline is at a relatively low angle to the board (30 degrees or so) and gently draw the saw backward for a few teeth. Because the teeth are designed to cut aggressively on the push stroke, pulling backward is an easier way to start a kerf. Once you have the kerf started, gently push the teeth forward in the kerf with the sawplate square (use a try square on the board's face to check if you're unsure).

Once your kerf is established, the saw will want to continue the trajectory it is on, so be careful that you don't wander off course. If the sawteeth are sufficiently set (angled side to side to make a kerf slightly wider than the plate), the saw should glide freely without rattling around or binding in the kerf. Follow the line across the board with the toothline at approximately 45 degrees (although you should experiment with your sawing angle to experience the difference between higher and lower angles).

On some boards, the kerf will close up and pinch your saw. You can gently open the kerf with your fingers, or for more serious situations, insert a wooden wedge into the beginning of the cut. Assuming that this is not caused by a problem with your saw (insufficient set), boards that do this either have too high a moisture content or have tension within them that is releasing as you saw through. A kerf that pinches is sometimes a sign of unstable wood, but don't discard the board just because it's cranky. Just keep an eye on it – it may move around on you after being worked.

An alternate position for sawing is to put your left foot on the board in place of your left knee. This puts you in a little more awkward body posture but it enables you to exert more power in each stroke.

As you make your way across the board, you will find dust piling up on the line ahead of you. Even though most of the dust will be pushed by the teeth down to the floor, enough will come up to be a nuisance. Blow the dust off the line as you saw so you can see where you're going.

As you approach the end of the cut, reach over with your left hand to support the offcut from dropping prematurely. Don't lift or twist; just support it.

As the last stoke is made, the offcut will fall into your hand (as shown above). It's bad form to let large offcuts drop to the floor, even if it's kindling. If you let it fall, there will be a greater likelihood of breaking out the last few fibers, which is not a practice you want to foster.

Here is an example of minor breakage at the very end of the cut even though the board was supported to the last stroke. Sometimes it's unavoidable, but you should always work to minimize it.

Crosscut the opposite end of the board to length. Unlike machine saws, handsaws make tiny shavings which are heavy enough to drop to the floor instead of becoming airborne. There's no need for dust-collection in a hand-tool shop.

This is a rough cut, never intended to be a finished surface. And although you want to aim for a square edge, these early steps are all approximate. Don't beat yourself up if your cut got wonky. As I showed in *Joined*, we never use the end grain as a reference surface.

Coarser crosscut saws will break out the bottom of a cut. It's ugly, but not irredeemable. This will disappear once the board is planed.

Use the rigid back edge of a knife to break off the shards before planing. Handle it carefully or you might later find yourself pulling slivers from your hand.

At this point, let's walk through the rip cut. Off a straight edge, scribe a line with your gauge set to the desired width. I recommend planing a clean edge on the board and setting the gauge to the exact width you need – you'll be sawing outside the line anyway. If you recall, the extra length we added earlier is an important step because the very beginning and ending of the plane strokes can be a little bumpy, but the width is not affected by this dynamic. At the risk of sounding repetitious, always scribe the *exact final width* – don't bother making this wider than necessary.

Scribe with the pin gently using multiple passes, progressively deeper each time. If you press the pin down too hard, it will follow the wave of the grain instead of the board's straight edge. This is a common mistake new woodworkers make – they try to gauge the line in one or two passes. It should be more like four or five.

Hang the board off the edge of the sawbench with your scribe line within an inch or two of the bench. Starting the kerf in a rip cut is the same as the crosscut – but considerably more awkward. Those big 1/4" sawteeth take a delicate touch to get going where you want them going. The key to success is practice. I recommend a practice session or two in which you work on starting rip kerfs on the end of a board. It doesn't use up much material, and many find it a tricky skill to get the feel for.

This beast of a saw is hungry and things can go wrong quick if you're not careful. I recommend you start by sawing outside the line by at least 1/8". If woodworking is a new craft for you, you might even leave more leeway. There's no shame in leaving a little too much. A heavily set plane can take 1/8" of material down to the line in a few passes. Once the kerf is started, you're off to the races.

The key to successful ripping is maintaining a steady rhythm while staying parallel to the line. "Let the saw do the work," we say. What this means is that your job is to keep the saw straight, to change the angle of the teeth when needed, and to make each stroke. But don't muscle it – the weight of the saw (and your arm holding onto it) does the work of cutting. There is no "proper" saw angle for ripping – the handle should be lowered or raised whenever it's called for. Lowering the handle (and therefore the toothline angle) assists your ability to saw in a straight line. This is partly because you can sight the sawplate along the line, but more significantly because there is more sawplate in the kerf. Raising the handle (and toothline) enables you to take aggressive strokes but can send you off course if you're not careful.

In fact, you can use this to your advantage in times when you need to steer a wandering kerf back to the line. In those cases, stop sawing as soon as you see the trajectory heading in a bad way. Raise the handle so that the toothline is perpendicular (straight up and down) to the board and gently saw while twisting the bottom of the saw's handle in the direction you want the kerf to go. It's best to do this with the toe of the saw, because the more plate there is in the kerf, the harder it will be to change course. So, yes, a wandering kerf can be corrected, but an ounce of prevention is worth a pound of cure. Keep your eye on the line.

Once you're halfway, flip the board over and saw from the other end to meet in the middle.

This is quick work in softwood. Each stroke of this beastly saw takes about 1" of material. At two strokes per second (a decent clip), you can begin to envision that ripping isn't the crazy arduous thing it's made out to be. Hardwood and thicker planks obviously require greater exertion, but once you get the hang of ripping 1" softwood, you'll be primed for the next level.

Experiment with the angle of the saw to find what's most effective for you, but make sure you've set your sights on connecting with the first kerf. The saw will do the cutting, but you need to do the steering.

As the saw approaches the first kerf, you will find the kerfs touch on the top well before they do on the underside. This is because of the sawing angle.

Here's the underside of the board in which the kerfs are touching on top. Ripsaws push the grain rather than slice it. This produces a telltale fiber string on the underside of the cut. The ripped fibers dangle, and all that's holding the pieces together is that 2" of remaining material between the kerfs.

Support the offcut and take the last few gentle strokes to finish the cut.

This saw is all about roughing the boards to size. It's not a pretty surface, but nothing your plane can't address in a few passes.

Boards of shorter length can be ripped in a front vise using the same process. I find dropping to one knee comfortable enough for these short rips. I also rip standing at the vise, but this position presents the toothline perpendicular to the board. It's fast; sometimes a little *too* fast. You've got to keep your wits about you.

Planing Rough Boards

Once your board is sawn to size, it's time to thickness and smooth it. (You ate your Wheaties this morning, right?) Although this may seem like such a pedestrian task to write about, I've come to believe that planing rough stock by hand is one of the most misunderstood woodworking operations today. Even a passing mention of planing rough-sawn stock by hand tends to be a land mine in mixed company. There will be just as much hissing and booing as there is chest puffing and gloating. But if we can be sure about anything in the kerfuffle, it is that handplanes are *not* neutral territory.

On the one hand, there are the *engineer woodworkers* – the ones who have made it their special focus to devise (or purchase) ingenious mechanisms designed to relieve toilsome or painstaking labor. These folks shudder to think of enduring the agony involved in handplaning a board to thickness. *(Oh, the humanity!)* They see how quickly machines can spit out boards with exacting precision and cannot imagine the time it would take to replicate that degree of precision with a piece of steel in a clunky block of wood.

Then there are the *monastic woodworkers* – the ascetics – who, in veneration of the spiritual mystique of hand tools, embrace the pain on the path to exactitude. For them, not only is the journey the destination, but they seem to hope the road never ends. They take a deep pride in taking the time to "do it right" – that is, they mean, as precise as humanly possible, no matter the time invested.

From my vantage point, both the engineers and the monastics make the same mistake: They assume that machinelike precision and regularity is the ultimate aim of woodworking. This belief implies that the degree to which furniture components deviate from the machinist's square is the degree to which the artisan has fallen short. *Sinned*.

But since when is the machinist's square the standard for "true" craftsmanship? Whence comes the law that smoothing plane shavings should be measured in "thous" and thou-shalt-nots? Why is the artisan's eye no longer to be trusted?

This common misunderstanding gets at a fundamental issue related to the future of hand work. I've become convinced that if we are going to successfully revive pre-industrial tools and techniques, we are going to have to understand and come to grips with pre-industrial tolerances. We need to know how square our "square" ought to be and exactly how smooth is "smooth."

When a machinist's square is placed on the surfaces of period furniture, one is hard pressed to find anything we moderns would call "flat." Even discounting instances of warpage from the ravages of time, the surfaces of rails, the flats of tapered legs, drawer faces, and even tabletops display a refreshingly human workmanship. It no longer surprises me to find that the undulations on a "flat" drawer face allow even my thickest feeler gauge (0.025") to freely slide underneath a straightedge. In practice, the wider the board is, the more acceptable these extremities of variation will be. An edge joint requires exacting standards, but the taper of a table leg only needs to *look* straight.

And that is, by the way, the only legitimate and sensible (in the most literal meaning of the word) measure of any surface that has no more than aesthetic concerns: Does it *look* flat, or smooth, or lovely? If it does, then it is. So, let the exercises in this chapter be an opportunity to train your eye and trust your fingertips to tell you when enough is enough. Leave the Starrett in the tool chest and learn to embrace *sensible* tolerances.

First, a quick lesson on adjusting wooden planes. One of the major selling points of these tools is the simplicity of their adjustment. All a person needs to learn is the three places to tap to move the iron up and down and side to side. The good news is that there is no mysterious guesswork in this process.

To install the iron in the plane, hold the stock in your left hand with your index and middle fingers across the mouth. Slide the iron down the bed (bevel down) and rest the edge on your fingers. Then, slip the wedge into position on top of the iron and give the wedge a confident tap to lock it in place. Don't panic about cutting your fingers – as long as you don't slide them back and forth, you won't do harm.

Take a moment to measure the projection with your fingers. Try to memorize what you're feeling. Now give it a pass on a piece of scrap wood to see what it does. If it's too deep, it is simplest at this point to re-tract the wedge and reset. Hopefully, though, your iron does not engage the wood yet. If this is the case, it's time to advance the iron.

Advancing the iron is as easy as it is obvious – gently tap on the top of the iron. I've come to use a regular claw hammer for this. The modern fear of "mushrooming" the top of the iron seems not to have been shared by many period artisans because it is common to find the tops of irons curled over from years of gentle taps. This phenomenon has been some-times mistakenly attributed to non-craftsmen overzealously beating on their grandfather's old planes, but its prevalence on surviving examples suggests otherwise. It is also worth noting that Joseph Moxon, Peter Nichol-son, André-Jacob Roubo, and Walter Rose all describe using a steel hammer for plane adjustment. I have yet to find a period warning against this practice.

Every time you advance or retract the iron, it's a good idea to give the wedge a little tap, too. As you make each adjustment, place your index and middle fingers on the iron to feel its movement. This is important feedback. Now take a pass to see what you've got. Continue advancing the iron until you begin to make shavings.

Once you begin to get the faintest shaving, examine which part of the iron is cutting. If the edge engages at one side and not the other, the iron is not quite square. To correct this, tap the top of the iron left or right. For example, to advance the left side of the edge, tap on the right side of the top of the iron. If you remember that the wedge functions as a pivot point, then visualizing which side to tap is easier. If you tap the wrong way, don't sweat it – just tap it back.

When making fine adjustments to irons with very little camber (such as in a smoothing plane), it is helpful to swipe a small scrap of wood across the iron's edge to make little shavings at the middle and sides to see the difference in the thicknesses. This method will easily tell you if you ought to advance the iron or if it is out of square.

And believe it or not, you can back the iron up the bed without completely starting over. On large planes, such as fore or trying (a.k.a. "joiner") planes, use a wooden mallet to give a smart rap just ahead of the throat (where there is sometimes a wooden insert called a "strike button"). Make sure you do this over the bench if you have a single-iron plane, because it loosens the wedge and can send the iron out of the mouth to the floor if done carelessly. Smoothing planes can also be adjusted by striking ahead of the throat but doing this on the end grain of the heel is preferred.

This retraction works because the inertia of the wedge and iron tend to resist motion as the body is shocked downward or forward. Subtle retracting adjustments can be hard to predict, but if the iron goes too far, you can always tap it forward again. In general, I think of advancing the iron forward as a slow, steady process and retracting almost as a reset.

Before you take a pass, assess the condition of your board. Does it rock on the flat of your benchtop? Is it cupped? Press on all corners and edges of the board to find where it's rocking. Make a mental note.

If you need to see how much cupping there is, feel free to check with a straight edge (a plane sole, try square, or other tool). Move down the length of the board to see if it changes at all from one end to the other. You are still getting to know this board, so pay attention to details.

Place the crowned side up against your bench hook and plane the hump out of the middle with your fore plane. Spread your feet wide (think power stance) and let your hip rest against the front of your bench. Handplaning is a full-body activity that depends on core strength. Most beginners stand with their feet close together and hunch directly over their plane, engaging little more than their biceps. This is a really great way to exhaust yourself and do substandard work.

Instead, broaden your stance and engage your core. Each pass begins by balancing the pressure on the plane front and back. At the beginning of the pass, your left hand presses the toe end of the sole firmly onto the board. The right hand's primary job is to push the plane forward (although it does slightly push down as well).

As the plane reaches the far end of the board, the downward pressure is shifted to the right hand on the tote. This avoids digging deeper at the end of a plane pass because the flatness of the plane's sole is registered to the board's surface. (Yes, this is why this tool is called a "plane" – it creates a flat plane.) Another way of thinking about this hand-pressure transition is to envision pressing the sole into the middle of the board. For some folks, this mental image helps them to maintain an even pressure along the length of each pass.

Check your progress with the handiest straight edge you have: your plane sole.

This rough approximation of flat is accurate enough at this point to proceed with planing the rest of the board's surface. The unmistakable camber of fore-plane marks can be seen in the light under the plane's edge.

At this point, the board no longer rocks on the bench when the (formerly) crowned side is down.

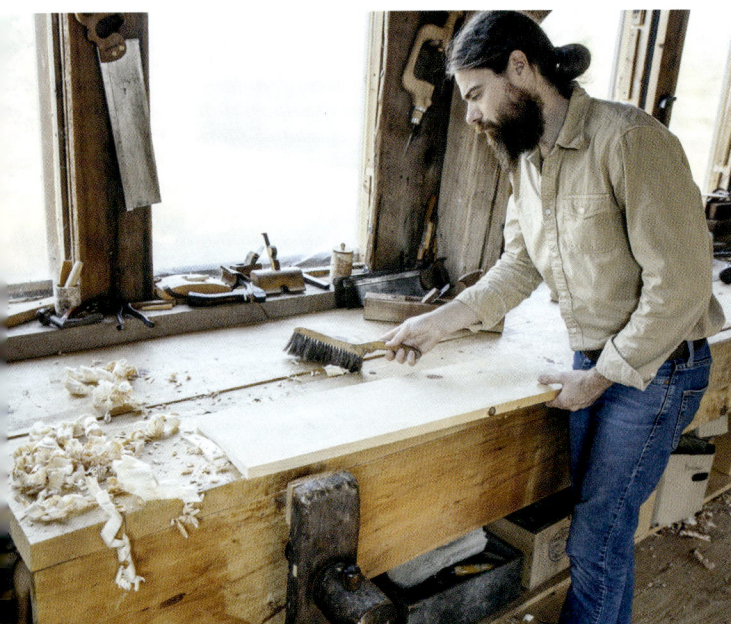

Although I often plane the rest of the surface as demonstrated so far, there are occasions when it makes sense to plane across the grain. This "traversing," as Moxon called it, can be seen in the secondary surfaces of period work. By slicing across the grain, heavy bites can be taken while minimizing the risk of major tear-out. Brush the shavings off your bench before shifting gears.

There are many ways to secure the far edge of a board for traversing: You can employ temporary battens, you can use holdfasts, and you could even use a tail vise. The most versatile and no-fuss way I know of is to utilize a simple drop-in peg system. I cover this system in more detail starting on page 118, but for now, suffice it to say, I drop a couple tapered pegs into holes. In conjunction with the bench hook, these three points of contact provide ample resistance to cross-grain planing.

To prevent breaking out ("spelching") the back edge of the board, plane a quick chamfer on it. The traversing begins at one end on the near edge and progresses across the grain down the length of the board. This is most easily done on a concave face because it gives your plane sole two points of contact, instead of only one high point of contact on a convex surface. Be extra careful to maintain even pressure, because your plane does not have a lot of surface contact to function as a reference.

The cross-grain shavings clearly show how the iron severs the long fibers of the grain. This is why tear-out is minimal.

As you take multiple trips down the board, the mountaintops (high points) will be brought down to the valleys (low points). This hollow in the middle will become progressively narrower until it disappears altogether. At that point, it's as flat as your plane's sole.

This is a completely traversed board. Assuming this is not to be used as an interior surface, we will take this further with finer cuts made lengthwise.

Here's the major problem with knots: tear-out. I could have demonstrated on some really nice mild-grained stock, but that would show very little of value. Instead, I chose a less-than-ideal board to demonstrate some of the ins and outs of dealing with hair-pulling trouble areas. These are the kinds of boards you get in real life.

This is what the inside surfaces of even some of the most high-style period furniture look like. No joke. It's par for the course.

With the iron set for a finer cut, clean up the fuzzy surface left from traversing. The best way to discern grain direction is, hands down, to take a gentle pass with a plane. There are grain-reading strategies that woodworkers pass around (I will show you the most reliable one soon), but the only *sure* method is planing. This is because the notion that every board has "a" grain direction is a myth. Most boards have all sorts of grain directions – the grain swoops and dives, confounding every theory and rule of thumb. Remember, trees grow in nature, not in laboratories.

So, work cautiously, especially around knots. If you get tear-out, that spot needs to be planed from the other direction. Flip the board and deal with that one spot in isolation.

Low, raking window light brings out the tool marks. This is an important point that I can't emphasize enough. Overhead lighting makes seeing what you're doing nearly impossible. If you can't situate your bench by a window, use a bench lamp to cast raking light across your benchtop.

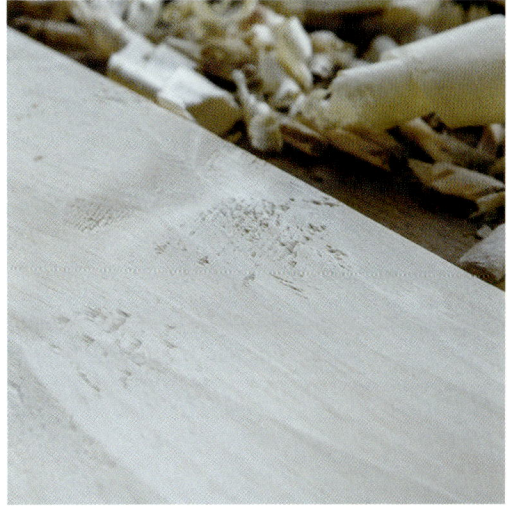

LEFT: A localized section of tear-out thanks to a sudden swirl of the grain. This will have to be dealt with by planing in the opposite direction only in that particular spot. It requires a deft touch.

RIGHT: This is all the smooth that's possible with a fore plane in this circumstance. Further refinement will have to be made with the smoothing plane.

LEFT: The tear-out at the far side of a knot is maddening to deal with.

RIGHT: Here's as far as I can get with the fore plane. Smoothing plane to the rescue...

By this point, you should be pretty well acquainted with the idiosyncrasies of your board. You know each spot where the grain dives. You are also keenly aware that you got a little carried away on that one edge at the end. So, teaching you to "read" the board at this point may feel a bit late to the discussion, but greater sensitivity is going to be important during these last levels of refinement.

On flat-sawn boards (such as mine above) in which the grain pattern displays a distinct series of stacked arcs or "cathedrals," you can use these cathedrals like signs pointing the way.

It's a long, technical explanation, but just know that this works because trees grow in cones stacked on top of each other.

So, here's the rule: **Inside Out, Outside In.**

Let me explain... When you are planing the face of the board that was toward the inside of the tree, think of the cathedrals as a big exit sign pointing you in the direction to plane out. When you're inside the tree, follow the arrows out. It's the exact opposite when you're planing the face of the board toward the outside of the tree (as I am in this picture). In that case, plane against the exit arrows to go "in."

It really is as simple as if you're working the inside of the tree, follow the arrows. If you're working the outside, go against them. In this instance, based on the growth rings visible on the end grain of the board, I am looking at the surface facing the outside of the tree. That means I would need to flip the board end for end to plane those cathedrals without tear-out.

If you need a goofy visual to burn it into your memory, here's what I use: I picture a theater full of people filing out while the closing credits roll, following the exit sign into the parking lot. Shortly after, others begin filling the theater (against the direction of the exit arrow) for the next showing. *Inside Out, Outside In.* I told you it was goofy.

Anyway, try it out to see what I mean. I'm sure the model will fail you on occasion because boards like to do their own thing. But that's what makes woodworking so engaging.

So, we've covered flattening and cleaning up, but we also want to make sure the board does not twist down its length. For more than 90 percent of my work, sighting down the length of the board is sufficient to determine if twist is present.

I start by looking at the front end of the board (foreground)...

...and sighting down the length to the far end. By comparing these two ends, I can usually get a pretty clear sense of any problematic twist.

For unusually wide or long boards or components that require extra precision, I use a pair of shop-made "winding sticks," parallel-edged straight sticks used to highlight twist. My front stick has black ink on the top edge to contrast with the rear one. The extra length exaggerates any twist that your stock may have. Set a stick at each end and crouch down to sight them.

Comparing the stick in the foreground to the stick in the background clearly shows that this board does not have twist. Phew. (Also, you can notice in the light under the front stick how "flat" the fore plane's cambered iron can get us.)

Let your focus jump from the near stick to the far one. Also, move the sticks down the board to confirm there's no funny business going on in the middle.

On table rails and other small stock, I'd skip right to the smoothing plane and call it good, but if the stock is larger and flatness is of greater importance (say, as in a tabletop), pulling out a trying plane is a good idea. This 26"-long sole provides a greater degree of flatness.

Take fine cuts with the trying plane. This is mostly for smoothing and evening the fore-planed "flat" surface.

The trying plane has a slight camber to the iron, which can be seen in the shavings it produces. Notice how they feather out to nothing at the edges? That is because the curve of the iron cuts deeper in the middle. Camber prevents the corners of the iron from digging in, but it is also a handy functional feature in certain situations (see page 102 for this edge jointing tip).

OK. Now we can make those gossamer shavings that impress strangers at parties. Get out your smoothing plane for the last bit of cleanup.

In the tradition of Moxon's classic work *Mechanick Exercises; or, The Doctrine of Handy-works* (1703), by this point in your board processing exercise, there's little left to learn. After pages describing the use of the "fore plain" and "joynter," Moxon offers this brief comment about the smoother: "The *Smoothing-plane*...must have its *Iron set* very *fine*, because its Office is to smoothen the work from those Irregularities the *Fore-plane* made." That's it.

For the most part, this description is all you need. The planing techniques are virtually the same as you've been doing, only finer. I would only add a few comments. First, move quick. Don't do the slow-as-a-snail-hey-watch-this-pretty-shaving-emerge thing. Make quick, confident strokes and the majority of your planing headaches will go away. Second, try skewing the plane. I find this helps tremendously. Third, think of this tool as the "clean-up plane." You can spot-plane selected areas as you need to – there's no need to work in full-length passes.

The beginnings and ends of your planing work will likely show subtle stuttering and chatter marks. Don't sweat it – that's why your board has extra length. You can cut it off.

Smoothing is easier said than done, so you'll have to practice to get the hang of it. But that is what the pursuit of craft is all about: cultivating skill through practice.

The Hatchet

I know what you're thinking: What in the world does a hatchet have to do with furniture making? Based on primary sources, it turns out *a whole lot*, actually. Not only do Joseph Moxon and Peter Nicholson explain that the hatchet was a basic tool in the joiner's kit, but many period depictions of joiner's shops show a hatchet on a stump or lying on the floor to the side of the workbench. Joinery, being the trade responsible for crafting architectural woodwork (and occasionally some basic furniture), might be a surprising place to find a craftsman employing a hatchet so regularly. But Nicholson tells us that joiners "used [it] chiefly in cutting away the superfluous wood from the edge of a piece of stuff, when the part to be cut away is too small to be sawed." So, the hatchet is an eminently practical shop tool.

Let's see it at work.

In my shop, trimming boards to width is the most commonly employed task of the hatchet. When 3/4" of stock needs to be removed, does it really make sense to get out the ripsaw? What would you even do with that little stick? Hoarders might save it for glue blocks, but how much glue-block stock does a person really need to keep on hand? Another method is planing it all away. That makes sense for 1/4" of material or so, but any more than that and it's wearisome. For offcuts that are too small to be of any practical use and too big to simply plane, the hatchet is the way to go. Scribe your gauge line as if you were going to saw it (though scribe on *both* faces of the board) and walk over to the hewing stump.

If the grain is dead straight and you're feeling lucky, you can place the hatchet on the top of the board and split the bulk of the waste away like it's firewood. It's a risky move that I commend to those who need to live a little.

But if the planets are not quite aligned for you, begin your hewing conservatively. Observe the direction of the grain so you don't end up splitting the board beyond your gauge line. Start a few inches from the bottom and chop a small relief cut about half the distance to the line.

Keep your left hand's fingers well away from any hewing, although you need to make sure you've got a good grip on the board.

Then progressively move up the board at least halfway with more relief chops. The lower relieved areas will fall away as you make progress upward.

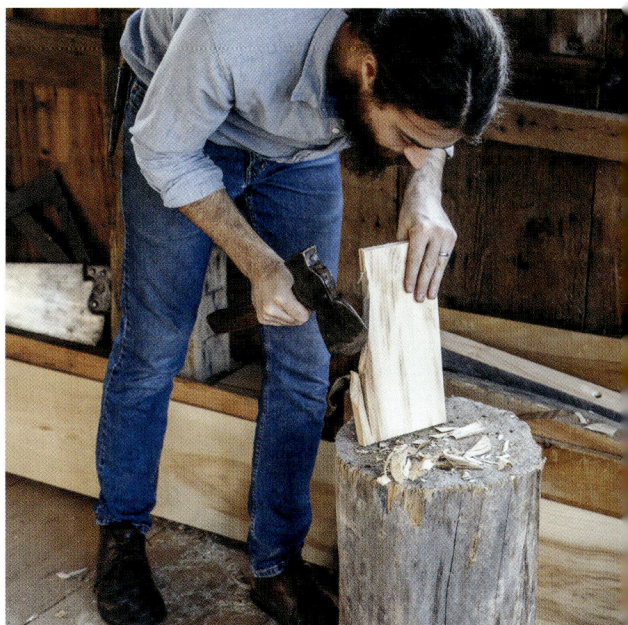

Get as close as you can to the line without overdoing it. Keep an eye on both the back and front of the board because some boards have a mind of their own.

Then flip the board and hew the remaining waste. Again, take little bits at a time and watch the grain closely. You may need to flip the board a time or two to navigate screwball grain.

It is possible to get quite close to your line in only a few swings. Truly, reading the description of this process almost takes more time than actually doing it. In regular practice, the hewing depicted here would rarely take me more than 30 seconds. Having the stump only a few steps from my bench encourages its use. It pays to get good with the coarsest tools – that's where your biggest time savings comes from.

A fore plane will take that last bit to the line in only a few passes. Overall, this is the quickest (and, by far, the most enjoyable) way to trim a board's width by hand.

There are other good uses for a hatchet. One of the most overlooked is starting wide bevels on panels or drawer bottoms. There is typically so much material to remove that starting out with a plane is a bit tedious. Hatchet marks can be found not only in early or "primitive" joinery work, but also in industrial-era cabinetmaking. I've seen drawer bottoms and backs with hewn portions on all sorts of furniture.

Start slow and take progressively deeper chops, making sure the stock is fully supported underneath (don't do this over a hollow in the stump). A steady hand can leave very little cleanup for the fore plane. Get good at this – you won't regret it.

This drawer bottom bevel shows clear hatchet marks. I think most woodworkers would assume this was a 17th-century piece or at least a funky vernacular oddball. In fact, this is from an elegantly grain-painted mid-19th-century bureau. The top-level workmanship and standardization of form suggests that this piece came from a rather prolific cabinetmaking shop, not some farmer's home shop. This is remarkable because it exposes the assumption that hatchets existed only in the purview of joiners and woodsmen.

We'll see more hatchet work in the next chapter, where we tackle green stock.

Riving and Hewing Green Stock

I wish we would not remain stuck in the mindset of segregating furniture making from green woodworking. Anyone who makes furniture should get comfortable riving with a froe and maul. Not only is it useful for green stock, but riving can be done with dry stock as well. This is an essential skill to have when you need the superior strength of dead-straight grain.

Green woodworking is an umbrella term that has come to describe the methods of work in many crafts, and as such its scope is truly enormous. I will not attempt any level of comprehensiveness here, but only offer a start that is most relevant to furniture making. Further instruction would include felling trees, riving large logs, using riving brakes, bending, weaving, designing with shrinkage in mind, etc. As I said, enormous scope.

This chapter will be focused on riving, hewing, and shaving stock for round chair parts. It's a good start and covers most of the basic skills for the thousand other rabbit trails that you may choose to venture down.

While large logs will be rived out in the forest or in the wood yard, smaller billets can be broken down in the shop at the stump. This piece came from my firewood log pile, now several months old. This means that this piece is not freshly felled, although because it had been recently sawn from the log, it retained a good amount of moisture.

Set the billet on the stump and place the blade of your froe on the end grain. Look for any major checks on the end of the billet and line up your split on that if possible. You want to split the billet into two evenly sized parts. With a hefty maul, take a whack on the back of the froe.

The split will start for at least a few inches.

Once you drive the blade to full depth, leverage the handle a bit to slide the blade deeper into the crack.

Once you're down in, a long froe blade turns out to be quite handy. Center the blade on the billet so that you can fit the maul on both sides of the piece as you drive the froe.

Continue attempting to leverage the split open. Once you see it begin to give way, you can set the maul aside and pull down on the handle to twist it open.

Depending on the species, a few fibers may hold on. Don't bother snipping fibers on a piece this small – let the froe do the work.

A simple flick of the wrist and the two pieces pop apart.

This one's got some twist. It's not a dealbreaker for chair parts, though. They'll be plenty strong.

Now, split the halves into quarters.

The twist is still present but hewing it round will not be a problem.

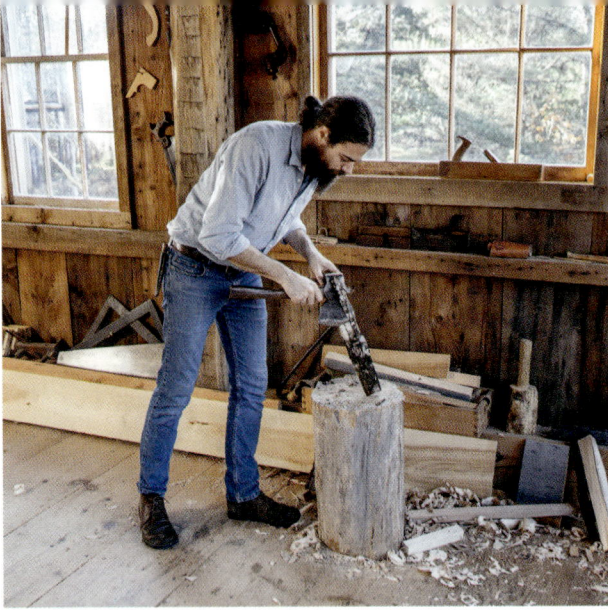

Slide any loose bark off with the hatchet so that it's not flopping around in your way.

Pick one corner and, tilting the stock back, begin hewing relief chops from the bottom up to about halfway.

Notice how my right foot is back for safety's sake. Also, my chops are not arcs that would swing down into my knee – instead, they are directly vertical, straight down onto the center of the stump.

Feel free to chop the lower material away as soon as it will give way without much force.

The relief chops do not have to be deep but it's better to do several tight together than spread apart.

Clear the waste away.

Rotate the stock to hew the other two edges to match the first.

Then flip it over and finish the three chamfers. From there, sight down the length of the stock and selectively hew bulges and high spots. You can also chamfer the chamfers to further the rounding process, if you like.

The drawknife at the shaving horse is the perfect method for finishing round stock, whether it's prepping for the lathe, or creating a final surface. The quickness of adjustment and the flexibility of use make this a valuable asset to any shop.

The automatic release of the dumbhead when I lift my foot off the pedal makes checking for humps and bends a cinch. This piece is ready for a chair.

Resawing

Sooner or later, you're going to need to make thin boards. Drawer parts and small boxes look clunky with the 3/4" and greater stock sold at lumberyards. If you make a desk, the pigeonhole dividers in the gallery are thin blades that will have to be resawn. And if you're really crazy, you can head down the sawn-veneer rabbit hole. There are *a lot* of great excuses to break out the ripsaw.

If you get your hands on 1-1/2"- or 2"-thick softwood, you've got more than enough thickness to saw yourself some drawer stock. Sides, backs, and bottoms are typically 1/2"-thick or less.

Let's walk through a basic resawing operation.

Choose a flat reference face on your board and run a marking-gauge line around the edges and ends, referencing off of that face. This line (which guides your sawing) should be centered in the thickness if you want two pieces of the same thickness.

Clamp the marked stock in your front vise, tilted away so that you can start at one corner. You will recall this sawing position from the tenon sawing (*Joined*, page 36). Orient your body so that your right arm is directly in line with the saw. You will want to make use of the entire line of teeth. Spread your feet apart for balance and power. Engage your core.

Use your thumb to start the kerf directly on the gauge line and begin sawing down the lines on the end and edge visible to you. Be careful to stay on the line because wandering off course will reduce the final thickness of the entire board.

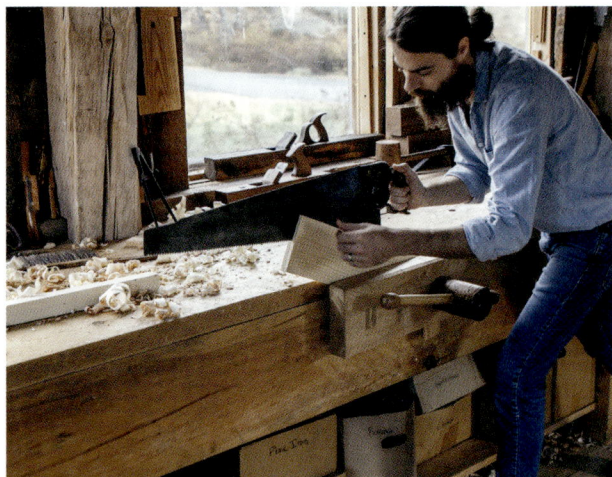

Play around with the angle of the stock to balance power and steering. When the stock is lowered like this, run the kerf down the edge a bit, even if it's shallow. Once the kerf is established, it is a lot easier to stay on track.

The saw is positioned dead center, which will result in two boards of even thickness.

Carry the kerf all the way down to the far corner of the end grain and the bottom corner of the edge grain. Make sure the waste between those two points is completely sawn away. This means you're half-way there.

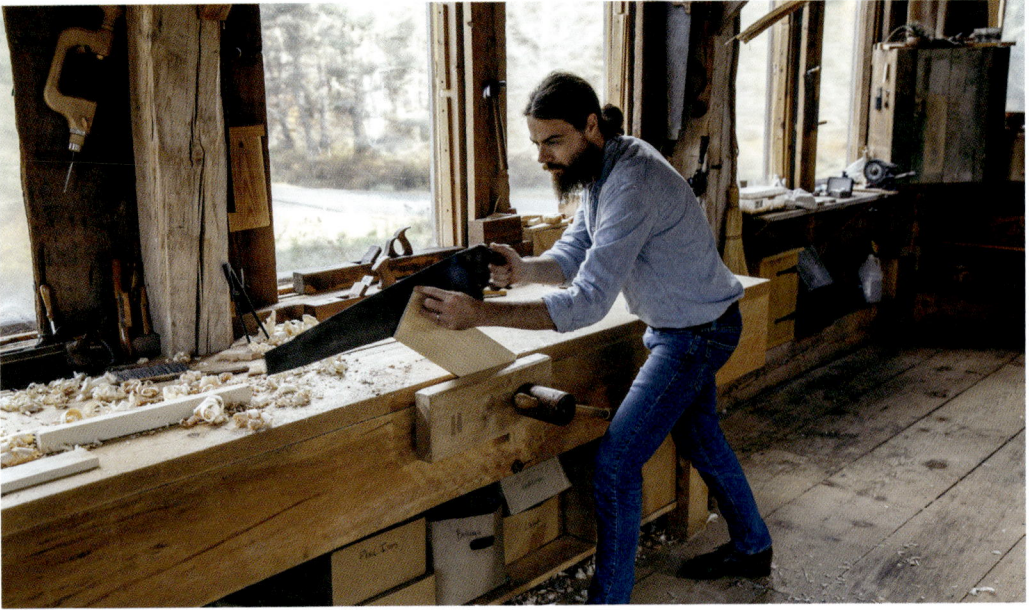

Flip the board over and begin at the opposite corner. I find it helpful to flip the board a few times and start at each corner. I consider the four corners the reference points that establish the flat plane created by the saw kerfs. Thought of this way, you start a cut at each of the four corners and simply connect those points to each other.

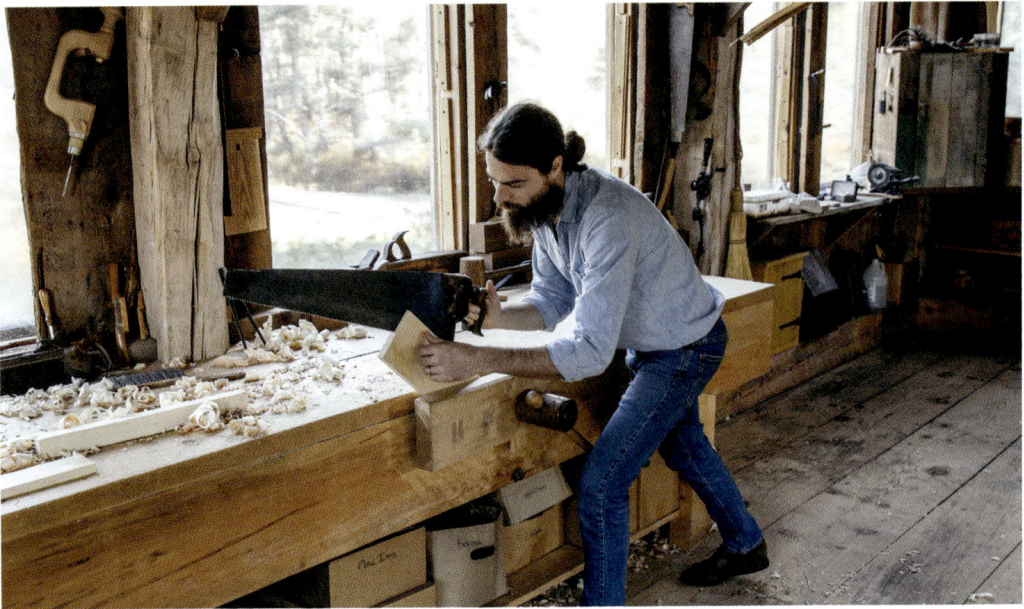

Change the angle of the sawing all you want – just don't let yourself stray from the line.

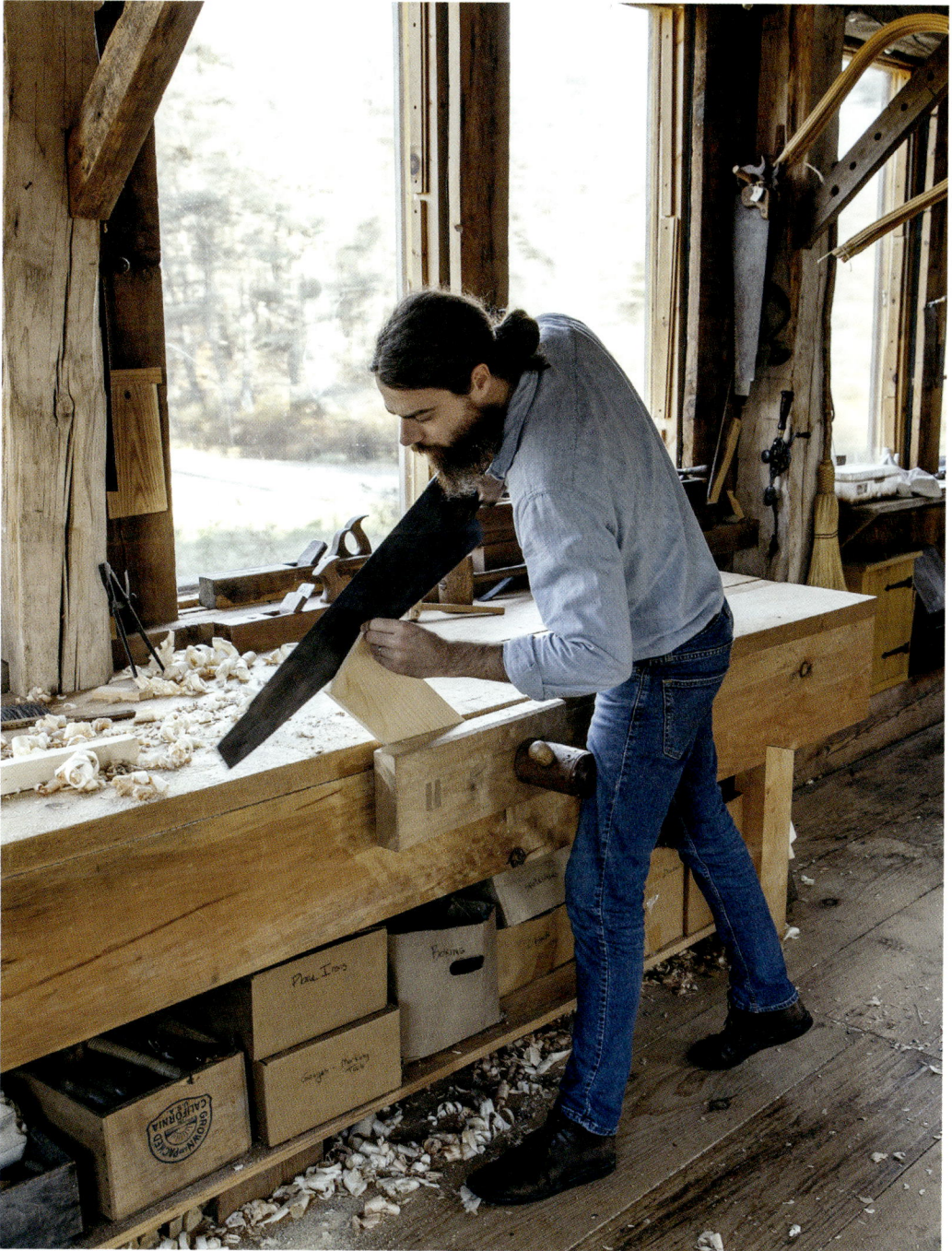

Establishing the end-grain kerf can be a little tricky, so take it slow. Lean over the work and pay close attention to your sawplate as you do this. Make sure you're not tilting the saw out of square.

Connect the kerfs as you work your way around.

Once you've made it all the way around, your pieces will probably be connected by a little bit of waste in the center. Stand the board vertically and saw them free. You have a good amount of sawplate in the kerf at this stage, so the risk of going off course is less.

Voilà. It's not pretty yet, but it only takes a few passes of the plane to clean up. This photo does clearly show my sawing pattern on the surfaces. Studying this may be helpful to inform your approach.

To plane thin stock, place a tapered board between you and your bench hook. This way you will not risk crashing your plane into the hook.

This extended stop can be seen as disposable and made on the fly as needed. On the other hand, if you need one of these on a regular basis, you can hang one under your bench for easy access any time. Just make sure it's tapered thin enough for the thinnest stock you will plane.

You can start with a fore plane as long as it's set for a light cut. It is easy to get carried away.

A smoothing plane can take the stock down to a gauge line set to the exact thickness you need.

Resawing is a relatively simple operation that every woodworker should practice to become comfortable doing. Commit to a project that requires it; you can use some offcuts to make a few delightful little boxes. Make sure you have this skill in your back pocket for when you need it.

Edge Jointing

Of all the tasks a woodworker could write about, edge jointing might be the most challenging. This is because the description of what has to happen is simple and obvious, but pulling it off requires an attuned sensitivity to subtleties.

Moxon's 1703 description of the process is illuminating: "[T]he Hand must be carried along the whole length, with an equal bearing weight, and so exactly even, and upright to the edges of the Board, that neither side of the *Plane* encline either inward or outwards, but that the whole breadth be exactly square on both its sides; supposing its sides straight: so will two edges of two Boards, when thus *shot*, lie so exactly flat and square upon one another, that light will not be discerned betwixt them. But yet it is counted a piece of good Workmanship in a *Joyner*, to have the Craft of bearing his Hand so curiously even, the whole length of a long Board; and yet but a sleight to those, [whom] Practice hath inur'd the Hand to."

It's that phrase in the last sentence – "bearing his Hand so curiously even" – that highlights the problem. The word "curiously" in the old sense means "carefulness, diligence, skilfulness." So, Moxon is essentially saying, "holding his hand evenly with careful skill." But, he concludes, it is easy for those who have accustomed their hand to the action.

So, practice is key.

The whole idea of edge jointing is to make two edges perfectly straight and square the entire length of the board so that they can be glued up to make one wider panel. There is another technique in which the craftsperson leaves the faintest intentional hollow in the middle so that only one clamp is needed for glue-up. This "spring joint" is a handy technique, but it requires the same degree of hand skill to execute, so I will simply demonstrate the traditional straight-edge method here. At the end, I will show one alternative method that is worth knowing about. You might ultimately prefer that one after trying both.

Start with a finely tuned trying or jointer plane. This should have a dead-flat sole and a razor-sharp iron. The key is planing with even pressure throughout the whole cut. Take light, full-length passes. This will progressively knock the high spots down until you are making full-length, uninterrupted shavings.

Don't press down too hard or it will be difficult to maintain even passes. Allow the weight of the plane to do most of the work, although the toe will likely need a little more pressure to make it even. Also, with the left hand, curl your fingers underneath the sole to ride along the board during each pass. This gives tactile feedback as to whether or not the plane remains square.

After you're taking full-length shavings, check the joint with a reliable straightedge. Crouch down and sight underneath to look for light shining through. Bob your head up and down a bit to change your vantage. You do not want to see any light. If you do, note that location and take another full-length pass with the plane. Do not attempt to plane only part of the joint – it will likely not go well.

Once your edge is close to dead-straight, check for squareness at multiple points down the length of the board. If you're way off, like this example, you will need to address it.

There are several ways to square up. One is to use a straight iron and shift a little more pressure on the high side of the plane. I find this method tricky to nail consistently. The second is to laterally adjust the iron so that it is skewed in the mouth, taking a heavier shaving on one side than the other. This is easier to do in metal-bodied planes with lateral adjustment levers. The method I prefer requires no adjustment whatsoever and no localized hand pressure: I just use a slightly cambered iron, offset when needed.

My trying plane's iron is cambered, which makes no difference to the joint when the iron is centered on the board. But, when I find one edge higher than the other, I simply shift the center of the iron directly over that edge. This way, the shaving fades to nothing on the low side due to the curve of the iron's edge.

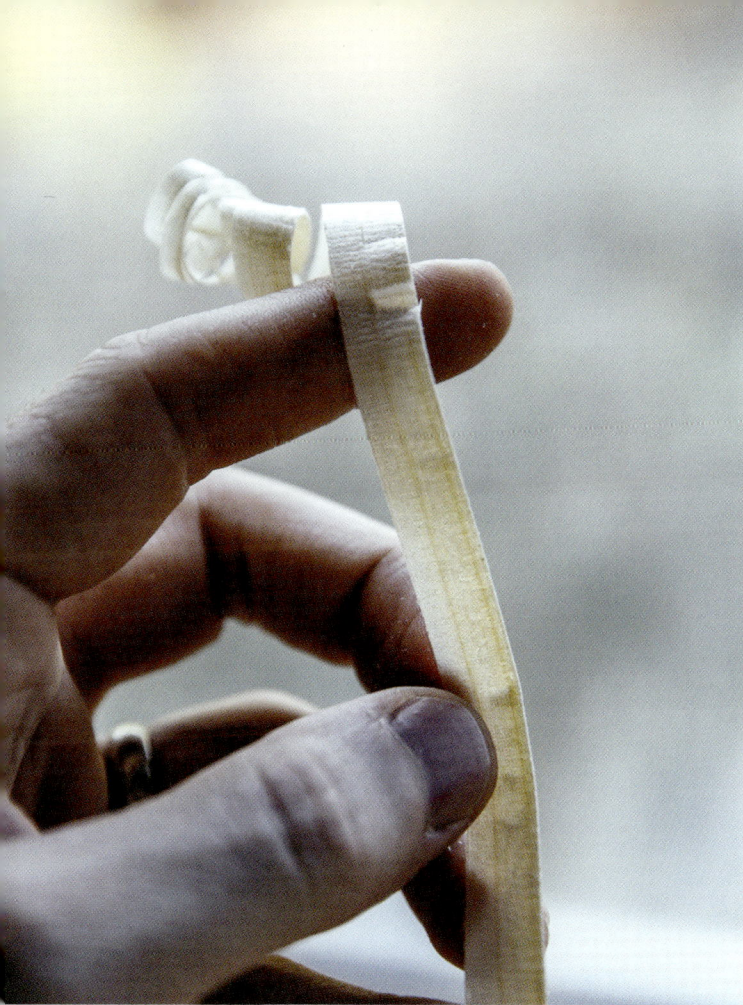

Here's the shaving taken from this off-center planing. The high edge was planed more heavily than anything else, and the iron never even touched the low edge.

After a couple passes with this technique all should be squared up. The trick here is to not undo your work from earlier steps. (As a beginner, you will find that once you square the edge, you'll check the length again with the straightedge and, darned if you knew it, now there's light under there again. You'll jump back and forth until you get both straight and square.) Next, repeat the process for the mating board.

When checking the fit of mating edges, place one board in the vise and set the other on top. Sight for light gaps on both front and back faces. Then, place a hand at each end of the top board, and test the fit by rocking or swiveling. This reveals whether it is in wind (rocking) or has a hump in the middle (swiveling). Make the necessary adjustments.

Remember, it'll become easy once you've "inured" your hand to the operation. Lots of practice. Or, you'll only use wide boards from now on.

OK, here's the other method I promised earlier I'd show you. This method planes both edges of the joint at the same time in order to eliminate the squareness variable. But there's a catch...

With both boards in the vise at the same time, you can plane a straight edge down the whole length disregarding square-ness. This will work out in the end because they both are planed at the same amount off 90 degrees.

When the two out-of-square edges are placed together, their angles counteract each other and maintain a flat panel. What a revolutionary idea, right? After all that sweating over straight *and* square, wouldn't it be a gamechanger to only focus on one of them?

Not so fast.

In my judgment, the benefit of ignoring squareness is nullified by the extra precision required in the straightening. Think about it: When the two pieces are planed together, if your edge falls off by .010" at the far end of the board, that amount will be doubled when you place the two edges together. Suddenly, your almost-passable low spot becomes a gaping tunnel in the assembled joint. So, even though you save on fussing over squareness, you double the fussing over straightness.

All in all, I prefer the first method.

SECTION II: WORKHOLDING

Both 'free' and 'restrained' workholding...

It's been said that woodworking is little more than marking lines in the right places and cutting carefully to those lines. While simplistic, there's something refreshing about the aphorism. It is true that knowing where and being able to cut wood is the heart of most woodworking operations. At the same time, in the shop, we are nothing without our tools. And our tools are nothing without a way to secure the stock being shaped.

Having a firm grasp on workholding methods is an essential component to artisanal development. Beginners struggle to find a way to hold their stock for comfortable work, and this struggle greatly hinders the cutting action of their tools. But anyone who's been around for any length of time has developed mastery over the material. When the craftsman says, "Sit," the board sits. When he says, "Stay," it stays.

There is quite a diversity of workholding methods from cultures around the globe. The majority of the world retains vestiges of traditional craft practice that utilizes what we around here at M&T have come to call "free" work – workholding that is secured against a single stop or in the grip of the artisan. The board can be flipped around, rotated, or examined in a moment and returned to position for working. It's not locked up in a vise or held down by clamps.

But vises also have a venerable, centuries-long history. Woodworkers have long utilized the screw to immobilize boards for sawing and shaping operations because there are some tasks that are just so much easier to accomplish at a vise. An efficient hand-tool woodworker will be fluent in both forms of workholding.

The methods I present here are those I employ regularly in my shop. There are many other (nearly infinite) clever solutions out there in the world because there are so many creative people with particular needs. But this book is not a showcase of novelty – it's a guidebook for efficacy.

So, take these methods as a starting place. Try to get comfortable with them then adapt them as needed.

In each unique circumstance you encounter, ask yourself these three questions:

1. What is the *simplest* way to hold this stock?
2. Is it secure enough to work *safely* and *effectively*?
3. Is it *quick* to release and adjust?

If you have affirmative answers to these considerations, you will be well on your way.

'Free' Work

In the majority of cases, woodwork is slowed when the workpiece is restrained in a device. The incessant tightening and loosening of a bench screw and the setting and resetting of a holdfast add even more motions to an already manually intensive activity. And because no one position is ideal for every possible approach of the cutting edge, frequent adjustment becomes a nuisance.

While there are situations in which it is practical to fully restrain a board (as will be discussed in the next chapter), I find them to be the exception, rather than the rule. This means that my vise and my holdfasts get relatively little use and the "free" workholding techniques shown in this chapter make up the bulk of my work. If I can find a way to secure the board against a single stop instead of locking it in a vise, the work goes smoother.

This is because constant adjustment breaks the flow of work. We all know what it is to "get in the groove" when everything clicks. The saw glides in the kerf like butter and the plane glides across the surface, taking silky shavings along the way. The assembled dovetails fit like they grew together. This "groove" is, of course, not unique to woodworkers. In fact, this experience can be had in all sorts of life activities, from music to teaching to cooking to engaging conversations.

This mysterious phenomenon has been studied extensively since the 1990s when psychologist Mihaly Csikszentmihalyi published his book, *Flow: The Psychology of Optimal Experience*. The basic idea is that when someone is "in the groove" or in a "flow" state, as he calls it, being totally absorbed in an engaging activity, they typically experience a deep sense of satisfaction and enjoyment. Csikszentmihalyi explains that to be in such a flow state, we must balance the challenge of the task at hand with our current skill

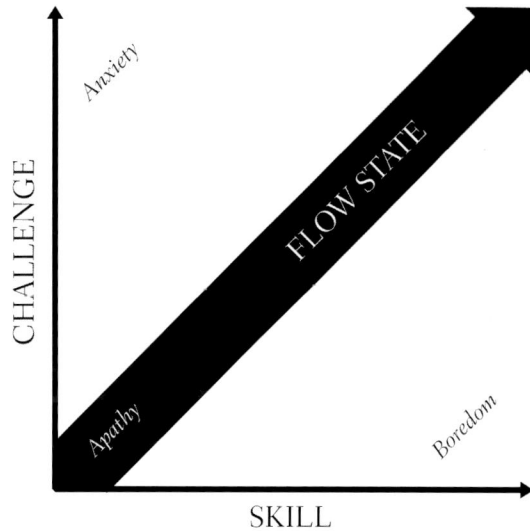

A chart with vertical axis labeled CHALLENGE and horizontal axis labeled SKILL. A diagonal arrow labeled FLOW STATE points upward to the right. Labels: Anxiety (upper left), Apathy (lower left), Boredom (lower right).

level. If the task is much too difficult for us, we will experience anxiety, but if it is well below our capacities, we will become bored. A rewarding engaged experience is found in progressively increasing the degree of challenge that can be met by increasing skill. The chart above depicts this.

Not only have I found working in the "flow" state to yield the most *satisfying* shop experience, but I also find it is more *effective*. Anything I can do to keep the work moving helps my mind stay focused and engaged.

When we experience these otherworldly floating-on-clouds moments of "flow," it's tempting to believe that the phenomenon must just be *happening to us*, as if it was a gift from the cosmos, totally outside our influence. We assume that on some days the planets are aligned and on others they aren't. But I'm not so sure. Over the years, I've found that I can choose certain ways of working that allow me to stay "in the groove," but there are others that can bring things to a grinding halt.

To my mind, there are few things more disrupting to the workshop flow than constantly readjusting vises and clamps. This chapter is intended to be a launching pad to inspire you to find ways to work more freely in your own shop.

Let's start at the most basic form of workholding: the bench hook – a wooden block (with or without teeth) fitted to a workbench against which a board can be planed or otherwise worked. The bench hook is most often mortised into the benchtop and its height can be adjusted according to need. It is common today to refer to this device as a "planing stop," though that name is of recent origin. In the Western tradition in which I work, this has long been referred to as a "bench hook," though it should not be confused with the modern bench hook that is used for crosscutting small stock at the bench (called a "side hook" by Nicholson). Utilizing a fixed block for working against is not unique to Western traditions – Japanese *shokunin* (craftsmen) used a similar block, though I am unfamiliar with its nomenclature.

I prefer the toothed variety. This hook has a blacksmith -made L-shaped iron fitted into it with teeth filed into the end for a secure grip. Though not strictly necessary, the teeth make a considerable difference.

Yes, the teeth leave a row of marks. Because your stock has extra length and will be trimmed, these will not appear in the final product. Unless you want them to – I've seen numerous examples of bench-hook marks on the end grain of period work. I find it quite charming, actually, in the same way I appreciate the signature undulations from a handplane.

Here's a look at my bench hook underneath the benchtop. It's a scrap of walnut tightly fitted into a mortise.

The hook is nothing fancy. Find some 2"-thick scrap and plane it square. Rough the surface for grip. I used a toothing plane, but sawteeth can provide the necessary crosshatch scratching.

Although I rarely remove it (or adjust the height much at all), the hook can be driven up and out of the mortise with a mallet. The fit is quite tight, especially in summer.

If you don't have access to a blacksmith, make use of an old-school (thanks, Peter Nicholson) solution: screwing a piece of old sawplate into the top of the hook. I used this one for years and it worked just fine.

I recommend mortising the plate into the top a bit so that the teeth can point upward. This ensures that the screw heads are lower than the teeth. You don't want the plane hitting the screws.

Here's another solution Nicholson suggests: "nails are driven obliquely through the edge, and filed into wedge-formed points." It is a gnarly look but seemed to work out fine in my initial experiments.

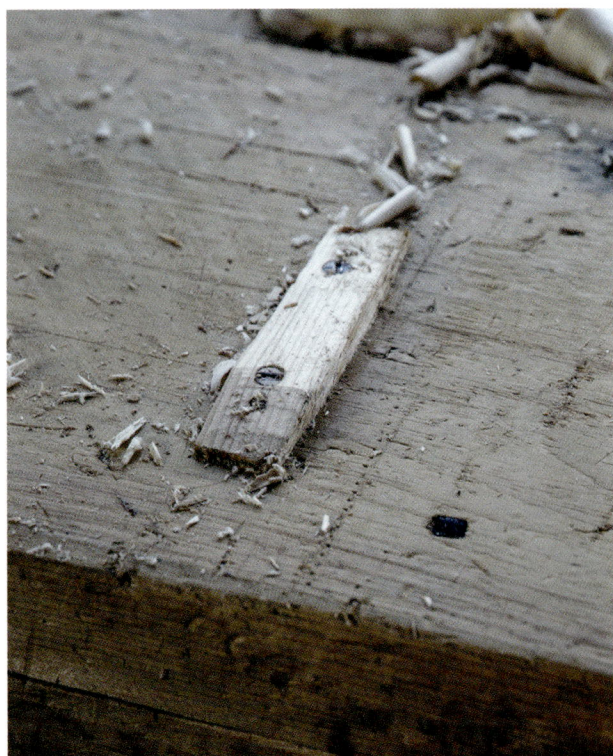

And one last option: a non-adjustable block fastened to the benchtop. This one is made of 1/2"-thick pine screwed to the bench. It gets regular use (such as was shown on page 48) and is quite durable. Worst case, one would have to swap it out every couple years. Although I prefer having the teeth of the first stop, this screwed-block approach is a solid choice. If you do not yet have a bench hook and just wanted to try it out, it's a low-investment way to start. I like having both in the shop. Options are always good.

Although the bench hook is particularly designed for planing, I've found it to be quite valuable for other kinds of operations. For example, marking stock. Most new woodworkers are surprised by the amount of finesse and control that is required to use a marking gauge. I mean, how much simpler could it get: Scratch a line with a pin? But the first time we try it, we discover it's not so simple. Between grain direction, the tilt and sharpness of the pin, and the amount of pressure applied over several passes, newbies can get frustrated. Because of this, it's important that the stock is secure when marking. Rather than depend on a vise, I find ways to hold it with my body. When one end is against the toothed hook and the other is against your chest (or gut), you'll have two hands free and the ability to make rapid adjustments on the fly. No patented "quick-release" mechanism required.

Every once in a while, a more concentrated planing force is needed and the board can get a little squirrely, sliding around with each pass. In those cases, try turning the end of the board into your hip and pin it against the hook. You won't need it often, but it's a handy technique to have in your back pocket.

I've rarely found a need for edge-grain (lateral) support in regular planing operations, but cross-grain planing does require a little more workholding aid. While many people use elaborate setups involving clamps, battens, and holdfasts, I prefer a less finicky approach.

We've already made use of the drop-in peg system in the planing chapter, but let's take a closer look at it. It is essentially a row of holes to hold pegs which support the far edge of the board. It's dead simple, infinitely adjustable (just add more holes), and so effective. There is no downside to this method.

I first discovered this system when studying the surviving workbench of Maine cabinetmaker Jonathan Fisher (1768-1847) and comparing it with the workholding arrangement depicted in a 1425 illustration of a Nuremberg joiner. I know that sounds obscure – so obscure that it probably seems impractical. I felt the same way until I tried it. After only a few minutes, I became embarrassed at my hasty judgment. This method is far and away the best.

I have a straight row of three 5/8" peg holes to accommodate the typical stock size I work with. You can add more rows for various widths should you find it necessary.

The pegs are made of softwood (why dent your board?), hastily tapered for ease of pulling and adjustment. These are *not* supposed to be friction fit. You want to be able to pull them out with your fingertips without straining.

Once the pegs are able to drop in easily, cut them at about 1/2" proud of the benchtop. That's just enough to offer support, but is short enough to stay out of the way when working with most any stock.

To get to work, all you have to do is drop the two pegs in their holes and slide the board up to them. Because they're tapered, they won't fall through, but they can be removed in a heartbeat.

So, if your bench hook needs a little lateral support, drop in a couple pine pegs. While this solution will never be the "hottest new bench tool of the year," I can assure you it is the best way to do this. If you don't believe me, give it a shot. What's a few holes and a couple quick pegs?

So far I've shown you the only two purposefully designed free workholding systems I use: bench hooks and pegs. But there are so many other ways to work unfettered by shop appliances. The key is to think outside the bench.

If you have your bench against a wall, you have many options available to you. I am regularly bracing the end of my work against the horizontal girt (timber) of my shop's frame. This gives full resistance without any setup. As a further benefit, working without the stock restrained forces you to develop accurate technique. If you're sloppy or careless, the board is going to shift around on you. When paring waste from half-blind dovetails such as these, I have to focus my cutting pressure where it counts, down and slightly toward the wall.

This is a great technique for clearing out rabbets too. It's quick to pop the chips before smoothing it out.

But remember that free workholding is a full-body engagement.
You can't just hunch over the board and push it up against a stop.
You have to spread your stance and lean your body into the work.
The more engaged you are, the better your work will go.

If you are working with short stock that is awkward to reach when pressed against the wall, block it out with scrap to bring the action closer to you. There are no limits to what can be done – you've just got to get creative. And remember the three questions at the beginning of this section: What is the *simplest* way to hold this stock? Is it secure enough to work *safely* and *effectively*? Is it *quick* to release and adjust?

Here's an example of exploiting the hidden assets of your bench's liabilities. When I made this bench, I wanted the depth from the front edge to the wall to be 30". I had a thick front plank and thinner rear board which, when set edge to edge, left me a 2-1/2" gap. Rather than look for new stock or glue up multiple boards, I decided to lay a strip between them that could be removed if desired. In my furniture conservation days, I used this kind of feature for clamping force on the inside of the bench, but more recently, I've found ways to use the filler strip itself as a stop. I've seen some really clever ways to build this into the bench, with a stepped thickness to adjust the strip's height. While I admire that kind of ingenuity, I find it simpler to shim it up with a scrap and pull it out when I'm done. Tips like this are not easily transferable to every work scenario, but I share it here to get you thinking about the possibilities.

Lastly, I would be remiss if I didn't confess my deep appreciation for my tail vise. I use this God-given, posteriorly located workholding apparatus to plop down onto my work for a sure grip. Not only does the booty clamp work effectively, but it's nice to take a seat once in a while. You'll remember from *Joined* that I sat at the sawbench on top of the table legs for chopping mortises. It's a real help being directly up over your work.

You can also sit while planing. Though it takes some getting used to, this board-straddling position puts a little more muscle into each stroke. A couple pegs (or protruding legs) function as stops.

And don't feel restrained by particular postures. Sometimes I crosscut stock with my left foot on the board instead of my knee. I particularly use this when I want more holding pressure (such as when working round sapling stock) and when I need to apply more force. Experiment with different postures and holding methods – there's really no limit to what you can come up with.

'Restrained' Work

I proposed in the introduction to this section that the efficient hand-tool woodworker will be fluent in both "free" and "restrained" forms of workholding. I hope that the "free"-work methods in the last chapter challenged you to think about new, flexible ways of working. But what about those times when you need both hands free, or just need that board completely immobilized? Thankfully, there are a handful of viable options. While there exist all sorts of innovative vises and clamps on the market, I will constrain my focus to the most effective, relevant, and basic of restraint methods. And because I use antiques, I'd direct you to the tool reviewers to get the lastest makers' names and compare their models if you decide to buy new.

Some tasks are just easier to do in a vise. Being able to clamp a board in place is a major asset when sawing joinery. Whether you're cutting tails, pins, or sawing the cheek of a tenon, it helps tremendously to keep that stuff still. It's possible to cut this joinery without vises, but it is much trickier.

Awkwardly shaped workpieces also need to be restrained. This branch door handle was too unruly for sawing comfortably on a side hook ("bench hook"). When it's held in the firm grip of the vise, all you have to think about is sawing. No wrestling required.

And sometimes, pieces are so small that it's hard to hold on to them any other way.

Let me introduce you to two forms of bench vises, both of which I highly regard: the leg vise and the face vise.

First, the leg vise. This vise has been used for centuries in all sorts of woodworking trades from cabinetmaking to boat building. It features a large single screw tapped into a front leg, which draws the chop into the bench's apron. All of my vintage bench screws have a thread pitch between 2 and 3 threads per inch. That's coarse. This is good because the coarser the thread count, the fewer rotations are required to open and close the vise. The bottom of the vise has a pinned parallel guide that provides counter pressure to the work secured in the vise's mouth at the top edge of the bench. The guide has a series of holes, allowing the pin to be moved to accommodate various thicknesses of stock.

Here's the parallel guide, mortised through the leg, with the pin in place. As you can see from the extra length, the vise can open quite wide, much wider than I've been tempted to use it.

The screw passes through the center of the chop and is locked into position by a small stick called a "garter." The garter rides in a groove in the screw's shaft so that as the screw is turned counterclockwise to open the vise, the chop opens with it. Without the garter, you would have to manually pull the chop open after loosening the screw. Garters save a lot of time and fiddling over the course of a project.

Also of note here is the softwood pad nailed to the inside of the vise chop. This arrangement was part of the vise when I purchased it (though I replaced the one that was there). I think softwood is a good way to go as it tends to grip a little better and does not dent the stock you're holding with it.

It's good to roughen the inside of the vise in order to increase grip. I used my toothing plane to create a crosshatch texture. I also do this to my benchtops because I don't like planing boards on a bowling-alley surface.

Next, my single-screw face vise. Featured in Nicholson's joiner's bench illustration, this vise operates on similar principles to the leg vise, although in a horizontal orientation. The right side of the vise has the screw and the left has a guide block that runs in a box under the bench, providing resistance to racking when the screw is tightened. It's not invincible and it racks some, even after a little adjusting. But that's life... rack happens.

This overhead view shows the guide. In some versions of a horizontal chop, the guide is substituted for a second screw. The double-screw method provides a more secure hold, but loses the benefit of one-handed operation.

Here's the garter on my face vise. It is mortised up into the underside of the chop and rides in a groove in the shaft of the screw (visible in the photo). I intended to pin this garter in place so it wouldn't fall out, but it's so tight that it hasn't budged once.

This is a small double-screw vise (sometimes called a "Moxon vise") I made for use on top of the bench. The screws pass through the front chop freely and are tapped into the rear chop. I've used this, held in place with a holdfast, for dovetailing wide boards and holding small stock upright for various fussy paring operations. While it serves its purpose, I have to confess that I haven't touched it in years. My bench vises do everything I've used this for.

Even the inside of this little vise is toothed – it makes a *huge* difference. In case you haven't caught on by this point, I recommend toothing *every* surface that you intend your stock to stay put on/in: vise chops, benchtops, aprons, etc.

There can certainly be a place for bar clamps in the woodshop, but nine times out of 10, the workholding scenario that might make us reach for a bar clamp can just as easily be solved with a holdfast. A holdfast is a crook-shaped bar of iron that clamps your work securely to the benchtop. It's old school – like *ancient* old school – and still outperforms the shiniest, priciest, Bluetooth-compatible bar clamps one could buy.

Here's a mock-up arrangement to show you how it works. The shaft of the holdfast passes through a hole (just a little wider than the shaft) in the benchtop, then the top of the holdfast is struck, which drives the shaft down into the hole. Because of the pad out on the end of the holdfast, the shaft is wedged diagonally in the hole, locking it in place. When your stock finds itself under that pad, it's going nowhere.

The hand-forged shaft is left quite rough for enhanced grip. Do not polish a holdfast shaft – you'd be asking for it to slip.

This is a 3/4" holdfast hole. In a softwood bench such as mine, the holes will wallow out sooner than in a hardwood bench, but it's nothing to lose sleep over. It'll be years of consistent benchwork before it becomes a problem. All the benefits of a softwood bench outweigh this single downside (but that's a big discussion for another day).

Using the holdfast is super easy. Slide the holdfast's shaft into the hole with the pad dropping onto the workpiece you would like to secure.

Notice how a softwood scrap cushions the pad so that it does not dent the stock. Having a caul such as this is important, not only for finished surfaces, but also for any surface that will ultimately become a primary (show) surface. The denting could be so severe that it would take a lot of planing to remove. Some holdfast pads are convex so no hard edges bite in. In my experience, these do not hold as well – and you want your holdfast to grip as firmly as possible. Some folks glue leather or cork under the pad or have fancy wooden cauls that are attached to the shaft in creative ways. This is way overthinking it. Just grab a scrap from the floor.

To tighten the holdfast, give it a good whack. When you strike the top of the arm with a mallet, it drives the shaft into the hole, which kinks backward and exerts pressure on the pad.

The shaft becomes kinked in the hole when tightened.

The tip of the pad should dig into the caul. The more the pressure of the pad is spread out over a larger surface area, the less well it holds.

Releasing the holdfast is as easy as setting it: Give it another whack. This time from behind. It will pop up out of the hole, ready to be reset. This is overall much faster than setting and resetting bar clamps, and it gives you clamping access anywhere on the surface of the bench.

Once released, you can see how hard the pad digs in. You don't want that on your precious board.

In summary, for the sake of efficiency, get comfortable using "free" workholding methods as much as possible, and if you need to restrain your stock, do it in the simplest and most easy-to-adjust way. By these criteria, the coarsely threaded bench vise and the holdfast are vastly superior to novel clamping arrangements.

Case Study: Tapering a Leg

Having walked through so many principles of stock prep and workholding, it's time for a case study. It's one thing to ponder how "one, in theory, would do X task," but techniques cannot be isolated from their context. Woodworking is, after all, about making *things*, not simply hand movements. Too often today, techniques are presented separated from the big picture, leading readers to assume that every board must go dutifully through every single step. It's this kind of decontextualization that leads so many modern woodworkers to assume that prepping stock with hand tools borders on insanity. "Why in the world would a person plane untold board feet to exactly the same thickness *by hand*?" we're asked.

I also wonder that question, but rather than point our furrowed-brow friend to the machine room, I would ask her, "Why is it that all of your boards need to be a precise thickness?" In 99 percent of circumstances, there is no good reason.

So, let's see what these principles and techniques look like in practice, in context. There is no task that better illustrates the mindset and work methodology presented in this book than tapering table legs on their two inside faces. This simple operation could be handled in many different ways, but it never needs to be complicated. Here's my sensible-tolerance, free-work, hand-tool-only approach.

First, take your already squared and mortised leg to the bench for layout.

Set your compass anywhere between 1/2 and 2/3 of the distance from the outside face to mark the width of the foot. Do this also on the opposite side, making sure that you are again registering off the outside face – it's easy to goof this up.

Mark the taper. Lay a straightedge from the inside of the bottom of the rail/mortise to the foot mark. Holding the straightedge firmly in place with one hand, use a knife or sharp awl in the other to scribe the line. Be careful you don't let the grain lead your line astray.

Do the opposite side. These two lines will guide you as you plane the waste away.

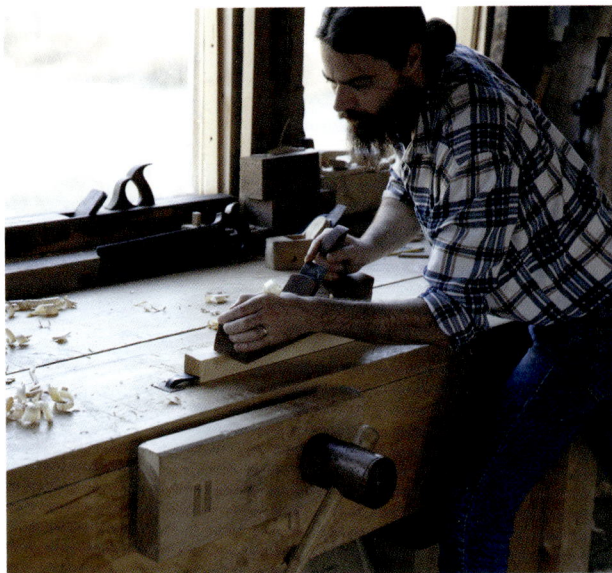

In softer woods, begin with a heavily set fore plane – it's coarse enough for this task. Butt the stock against the hook and begin planing short strokes at the foot end of the leg. At this stage, the cuts can't really be too heavy. Your physical strength is the only limitation.

As you get closer to the lines, bevel the cuts toward the lines on both sides. This allows you to keep an eye on each side independently. Once each side is one fore-plane pass away from the line, you can take the hump out of the middle to make it one flat plane.

At this point, you could use a trying plane to ensure it's straight, but I rarely bother. Just trust your scribe lines – it only needs to *look* straight. Your smoothing plane can take it from here. Sneak up to the lines – it shouldn't take much if you are just one fore-plane pass away.

Fairing the taper into the non-tapered top end of the leg is helped by a deft and sensitive touch, but it's nothing a little practice and good technique cannot handle. Gently set the edge of the iron at the taper transition point and rock the plane onto the toe end of the sole.

Press down firmly and take a swift pass. Once your scribe lines disappear, stop. You're done with that taper.

You didn't change your compass setting, did you? Good. Lay out the second taper the same as the first, this time from the other outside face.

For the second taper, I'll show you how I do this when using hardwoods: I hew the taper with a hatchet. Our method will be the same as the green-stock hewing we did earlier, only we're working to gauge lines. Take the leg to the stump and begin hewing the waste at the foot, being careful not to cut (or split) beyond the lines.

Hew stop cuts up the leg, progressively shallower to follow the taper. Don't try to do this on both edges at once – instead, make your cuts on both edges independently, just like you did when planing the two bevels to the lines. One errant blow can ruin your table leg.

Hew as close to the line as you can manage. If you're a nervous Nellie, go a little farther than you think you should. The key to efficiency is to let the coarsest tools do as much of the work as possible. Save your finely set tools for cleanup.

Your mileage may vary, but I tend to finish my hewing around 1/8" away from the line.

If your hewing was tidy, you can clean it up with a smoothing plane, but there's no shame in taking a pass or two with a fore plane. Work down to the lines and you're all done.

If you do these steps completely by hand, the leg will be imbued with a magical ability to stand on its own without any support. This is impossible to achieve with power tools.

Kidding.

SECTION III: WORKFLOW

These are the things you *must* get your arms around...

After reading the first two sections of this book and reading the instructions in *Joined*, some of my readers may be wondering, "How do I bring all these things together?" "What are some sound ways to approach the workflow of a furniture project?" These are good questions to ponder, and although circumstances vary, there are some general, tried-and-true principles that can be gleaned from the fruitful labors of those who have gone on before us.

This closing section is focused on the big picture of a project: how an artisan thinks through the process of sourcing rough lumber to prepping stock to cutting joinery to assembly. I offer here seven principles to work by. The list is not exhaustive, nor are any of the items necessarily profound. But they are the things that you as a hand-tool woodworker *must* get your arms around. This stuff is essential for hand-tool efficiency.

1. Forget the cut list.

Don't fall into the cut-list rut. While they can be useful as a general guide for ordering materials, I encourage you to develop greater flexibility. It's important to be able to adapt to the material on hand. If the plans call for exactly 7/8" finished stock, who says some pieces can't be a fat 3/4" or greater than 1"? Remember: All your joinery is referenced off the show ("sacred") face and therefore the thickness can be variable. And if what you've got on hand does vary, by all means *do not* plane all of your stock to exactly the same thickness – there is no reason to put yourself through that.

But of course, not everyone has their own stash of lumber on hand. So, if you're in the market, look up a local hardwood lumberyard. I'm sure you're not too far away from one – I've ordered several times from a yard three hours away from me. They deliver in my area every Tuesday. Alternatively, you can embrace the opportunity to take a mini road trip. Order a generous 50 percent more than you think you'll need. Not only are you accounting for waste, but this way you can begin assembling your lumber stash from the remainders from the build. Five projects worth of your "leftovers" and you've got yourself a sweet little cache.

But you should also check local classifieds. Craigslist has become a staple. Try *Uncle Henry's*, if you're up in my neck of the woods. Find your local source of bartering, dickering, and cash-only sales. You'll encounter barns of band-sawn oak slabs, stickered timbers sitting out in yards, and reclaimed pine boards from kitchen remodels. You'll meet fun folks and their dogs. It's always an adventure. Oh, and don't forget to bring *cash*.

I have to say that much of the wood I've used for furniture has come through word-of-mouth. Your wife's aunt probably knows a guy whose kids are helping him clear out his garage. He's got a pile of random wood and you'll get asked if you want some. You do. Go get it and put it in your stash.

Really, I cannot stress enough that if you connect with your neighbors and other local woodworkers, good wood will come your way. If you instead hide in your shop and never get to know anyone, you're cutting yourself off from the benefits of community. Your community needs to know you're a passionate woodworker. They won't call you if they don't know you. So, where to start? Maybe offer to teach a free kid's woodworking class on a Saturday afternoon. Sign up to do woodworking demonstrations at the town fair. Volunteer at the local history museum. These experiences and relationships are so rich that you'll forget about any other benefit. But then one day, people will begin pestering you with stacks of wood and old tools they want to go to "a good home." I am recommending that you work on becoming that good home.

2. Keep your stock under control.

So, you've got that stack of reclaimed pine boards and you're ready to build a six-board chest. Now what?

If your cache has grown to the point that you have it stored outside (stickered and under cover, of course), you're going to want to let the boards acclimate to the shop before working them. Ideally, you give them a week, but if not, you just need to keep them stable as you work them.

Boards tend to do funny things overnight. You can get a board planed dead flat at the end of the day, only to find it a Pringle in the morning. This is because a fresh planing releases some of the tension that was in the wood and allows it to move around. This is not a sign of defect – it's a characteristic of authentic wood.

So, how to work with/around this? Obviously, you ought not leave something as precise as an edge joint to glue up the next morning. But I'll sometimes even clamp regular flat stock overnight. If you have two boards that are already cupped, you can gently clamp them together with their convex sides touching while they acclimate to the shop environment. It's amazing what's possible with clamps and time.

My last bit of advice for environmental acclimation is that you should always do a test fit right before final assembly and, if you can swing it, assemble the joint the day you made it. Wood moves. It's best to pin it in place before it goes astray.

ABOVE: The inside of this 18th/19th-century drawer has a chalk "X" at the bottom edge in addition to an unidentifiable serpentine flourish.

ABOVE: The inside faces of this 19th-century drawer are numbered in pencil at each corner.

3. Label your work.

If the record of surviving period furniture says anything about shop layout marks and labeling, it tells us that everyone had their own systems. Although there were common themes, many organizational systems are so idiosyncratic that scholars see them as having "diagnostic" value when determining attribution – they know John Smith always drew that funny little semicircle on his drawer sides, making this "Smith" chest a dead ringer.

So, makers working outside of a strict guild system seemed to have come up with their own method to the madness. Over my years examining American period furniture, I've seen all sorts of cabinetmakers' marks: Xs, Vs, squiggles, numbers (both Roman and Western Arabic), letters, semi-circles in corners, etc. Sometimes these marks were made with chalk, but often pencil, and occasionally they were simply scratched with an awl. Just about any label you can think of has been done throughout history.

But what do I recommend? There are three things you're going to want to label/designate: inside and outside faces, reference edges, and mating joinery members.

Having seen a bunch of different systems, here's what I like to do: I leave the inside faces rough-planed so they can never be mistaken for show faces. The show face is the only surface that is planed smooth. The reference edge (assuming it will be hidden after final assembly) gets a single cross-grain scratch. Mating members such as tenons and their mortises get a cross-grain Roman numeral scratch: I, II, III, IV.

Alternatively, you can use a pencil, but it smudges. It's hard to lose track of an awl scratch.

ABOVE: This 18th-century drawer side is marked with a chalk quarter circle, which denotes the inside of the lower front corner.

LEFT: The dovetailed corners in this drawer are labeled with Arabic numerals. This joint is marked with an "8" which suggests that parts were labeled for multiple drawers at a time.

ABOVE: The top edge of the back of this drawer was labeled with a hash mark for reference during joinery layout.

ABOVE: The bottom board of this chest of drawers has a chalk inscription that reads "Bottom." The front edge was denoted with a chalk arc.

4. Use templates and story sticks.

Anyone who's been around woodworkers for a little while knows how valuable story sticks are. Rather than using a tape measure every single time for a repeated operation, making marks on a reference stick ensures consistency and saves tons of fiddling. I've used story sticks for dovetail layouts, locating chair-leg mortises, and turning details.

But don't view templates as tablets of stone; think of them as *guides* instead. Period Windsor legs were turned by eye, and a tape measure leg comparison (even within one chair) reveals the discrepancies. Templates are a handy reference, but you shouldn't feel confined by them.

5. Vary your tasks.

You are *not* a machine. So, why would you plan on planing boards all day long? Do an hour or so of planing, then tackle layout. Cut some rabbets. Spend some time riving and paring drawbore pegs. See what needs hewing. To keep your head high throughout all of this physical work, you've got to break up the operations.

And for everything there is a time and season. When that roast beef is settled in your gut after lunch, and you need to get the blood flowing again, plan some physically demanding work such as ripping. If the sun is shining and your energy is up, take that opportunity to break a sweat. Feeling in a calm and reflective mood? Touch up your edges. But don't save any task that demands your fullest concentration for the very end of a day or right after (or before) lunch. (There seems to be a lunch theme here.)

But is there an ideal order of operations in the hand-tool shop? Well, yes – in a way. I recommend doing in the moment whatever keeps you working strong. You are not a factory – you have freedom and flexibility to work on whatever you want, whenever you want. Don't get stuck feeling like you "have to" work on any given task at that moment. Take a break if you must. Above all, keep your spirit singing.

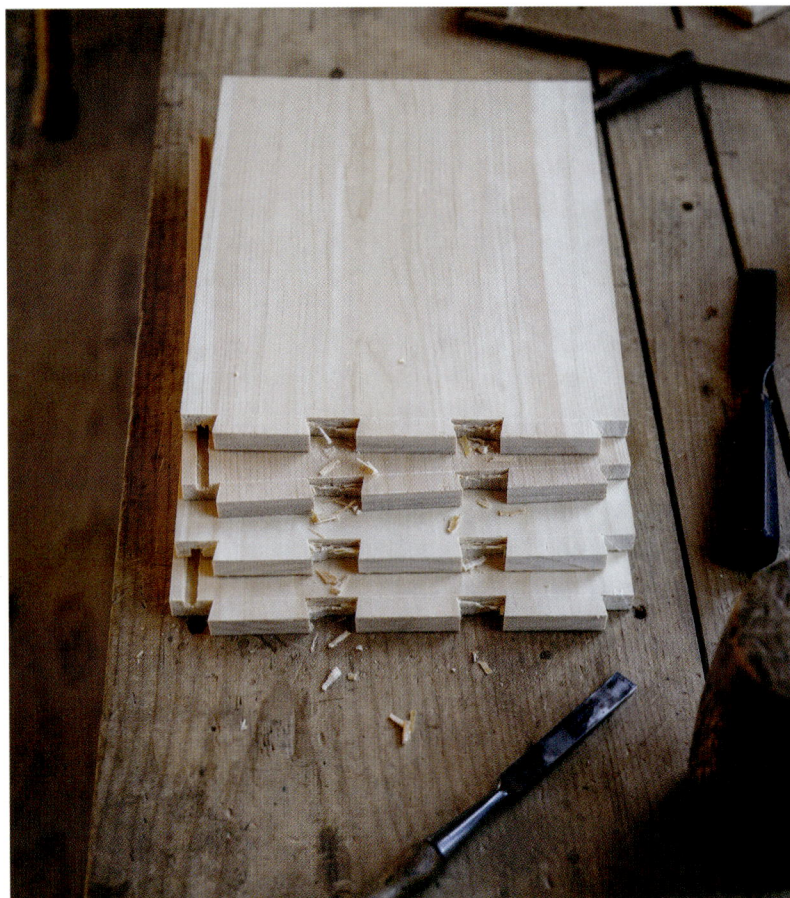

6. Work in batches.

If you're going to make one of something, you might as well make two. As I've been arguing in this book, hand-tool efficiency comes out of proficiency, but skill does not just fall out of the sky and into our laps. Repetition is key. We all know that our first crack at something can show that we're a little rustier than we thought. But if the skill has been developed, it only takes another try or two to get back into the swing of things. Exploit this.

For the sake of accuracy, it is a good idea to work through a small stack of dovetails in one session rather than jumping hither and yon. This is not intended to contradict the earlier advice to move to fun work when the task turns into a slog. The key is to balance the efficiency of working in multiples without it turning into monotony. I find a couple drawers' worth of dovetails is enough to get me into the groove. Move on after the first if you must, but harnessing that dovetail mojo might be worth taking on another drawer. You've got to find your own balance.

7. Make sub-assemblies.

Lastly, assemble furniture in stages to keep things under control. This is assuming that the entire piece is already completed, but it can be handy for those of us who have little time to see a project through to the end. Being able to assemble the two ends of the table and setting them aside might just be the ticket for you.

But even if you are ready for a one-fell-swoop assembly, do it in sub-assemblies. Do the front legs, then the back legs. Lastly, join the two together. This keeps the process of assembly calm and under control. This moment in the project is stressful enough already, so if you can distribute the stress over several iterations, it will go much better for you.

"**To *know* wood, you have to wrestle it.** To discover its secrets, you must take up the rough-sawn plank and **run a razor edge down its length.** There, you will find where the grain dives, how the board was oriented within the standing tree, and in what way the board's flat-sawn cathedrals direct you to **engage it.**"

other titles by this author

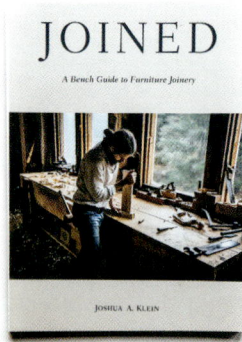

Joined: A Bench Guide to Furniture Joinery

Mortise & Tenon, 2020

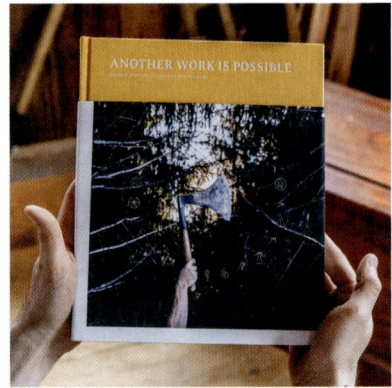

Another Work is Possible

Mortise & Tenon, 2020

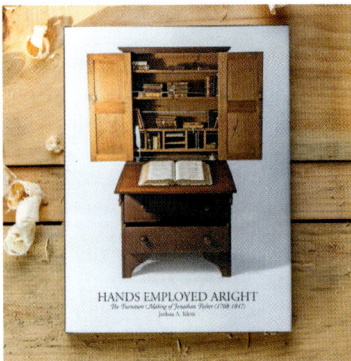

*Hands Employed Aright:
The Furniture Making of Jonathan
Fisher (1768-1847)*

Lost Art Press, 2018

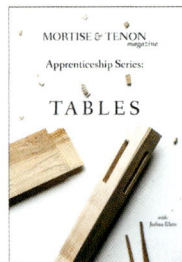

Apprenticeship Series
Instructional Video:
Tables

Mortise & Tenon, 2017

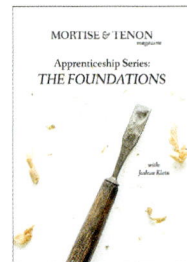

Apprenticeship Series
Instructional Video:
The Foundations

Mortise & Tenon, 2016

All available at:
www.mortiseandtenonmag.com

about the author

Joshua A. Klein is editor-in-chief of *Mortise & Tenon Magazine*. He has been selected for the Early American Life Directory of Traditional American Crafts for his authentic approach to period furniture making, and has presented about historic craftsmanship at museums around the United States. He has written articles for *Fine Woodworking*, *Popular Woodworking*, and *American Period Furniture*, and is author of *Hands Employed Aright: The Furniture Making of Jonathan Fisher (1768-1847)* (Lost Art Press, 2018), *Another Work is Possible* (Mortise & Tenon, 2020), and *Joined: A Bench Guide to Furniture Joinery* (Mortise & Tenon, 2020). Klein, his wife, and their three sons are currently restoring an 1810 cape on the coast of Maine.

colophon

Worked was set in Atlas Grotesk, a fresh sans-serif typeface that combines the style of the 20th-century European grotesks with the vertical proportions and spaciousness of the American gothics.

Printed by Signature Book Printing in Gaithersburg, Maryland.